The SavvyGuide to
Consulting and Consultancy skills

Adam Vile

AUTHORS Adam Vile
ISBN 978-0-9559907-1-7

Other books by Adam Vile in the SavvyGuideto series:
The SavvyGuideTo Grid, HPC, DataCache Cloud and Virtualisation(2009). With Jim Liddle. 978-0-9559907-0-0

Typeset in LATEX, printed by lulu press published by The SavvyGuideTo LTD

Acknowledgements

This is not the first book that I have written, and so I should have expected it to take up my time and energy over the weeks and months during which I have put it together. Even when you expect something, that doesn't necessarily make it easy and I would like to thank my family, Mickaella, Zoe, Matt, Bertie, Eloise, Alfie and Ophelia for their tolerance and support. A special thanks to Tess for her unceasing devotion to sitting on my feet and to Marmalade for her tenacity in getting me up in the morning. Thanks also to Jim for supporting me through the process and for his editorial help, and finally thanks to all of the colleagues and consultants with whom I have had the pleasure to work over the last fifteen or so years and from whom I have taken and repackaged nuggets of wisdom through this book. Too many to mention, you know who you are. You may even recognise yourself.

Introduction

I was trained to be logical. In fact I would have been a pretty poor mathematician without the facility for detailed and thorough logical thought. I developed a real skill for getting right behind and underneath an argument, to the extent where I could reduce anyone calling at the door, to convince me to buy or believe in anything, to a gibbering wreck (and sometimes even tears). If there was a hole in your thinking, I'd find it, and proudly (and quite smugly too) expose it to you and to anyone who was listening. This got me a reputation as someone not to be trifled with but it didn't get me many friends, and it didn't get me very far in my career. But I didn't care, and quite frankly I didn't understand.

I was working as an IT project manager in a large investment bank on a long project which was being made longer by the continued changes in requirements to the system that we were delivering. One day I trundled upstairs to my weekly user meeting with a usual list of illogical and irrational requirements fully prepared to demonstrate just how illogical and irrational they were, and to keep the project on track. I was good at that.

The usual arguments ensued, and I did well on dismissing them until it came to the point about the colour of a particular button on the user interface. Of course it didn't matter to me what colour it was, but as a point of principle I didn't want to change it. What I didn't realise was that as a point of principle, they did. I was stuck, no amount of logic could shift the user, she just wanted pale blue and that was it, there was nothing rational about it, and I just couldn't understand that. She started getting annoyed, then so did I. A colleague in the room uttered those words, you know the ones, the ones that have completely the opposite effect to that intended - *'calm down'* and in an almost Pavlovian response we both stood up and started a shouting match across the table. Red faced she shouted 'You never give us anything - Fuck You!! ' and stormed out of the room.

I had won a Phyrric victory. The button stayed pale green, but relationships with the users deteriorated to the point of obstructive unhelpfulness, I couldn't get anything done. The project was delayed, my promotion that year was stalled due to "objections from the users" and eventually I had to move to a completely new project with a new group of users, and start again.

As I left the room that day with my colleague he pointed out the obvious, that the meeting hadn't gone that well. And then he said something that made a significant impact on me and changed the way that I interacted with people for ever. He said:

> *'I don't know why you made such a big deal in there over something that is so small, lets face*

it, its not about logic and its not about being right (whatever that is) its about moving the project forward and getting support and buy-in, you just have to communicate better, its all emotion - the IT bit is easy. '

You just have to communicate better. I was a bit taken aback, annoyed actually (it wasn't a good time to criticize me!!) because I had always considered myself a good communicator. I had after all spent seven years teaching at school and University, what I didn't know about clear explanation wasn't worth writing down. But thinking about it later, he was right. I hadn't got across my message. All I had done was demonstrate that I was stubborn and petty. What I really wanted to say was that we were all under pressure to complete the project, and we needed to work together on the things that were high priority in order to hit the deadline. I realised then that my communication skills needed work. It took me a little bit longer to work out that my friend was right and that good communication was based more on emotional content than on fact.

Its all emotion. In the world of business logic is important for strategy and for establishing solutions but in order to get things done we need to engage in negotiation, influence, sales and management all of which are fundamentally concerned with establishing an emotional basis.

That day I started a personal journey to try to understand how to do my job better, essentially how to improve my communication skills. I read voraciously management books, books on communication, influence, presentation, project management and I attended business oriented courses provided as part of my personal gevelopment budget at work. I took something from each, but it wasn't until I took a week off to attended a course taught by Richard Bandler that the penny finally dropped. His approach to communication excellence (as he calls it) was extremely logical, yet immensely effective.

Bandler was a mathematician and computer scientist who achieved his Doctorate in linguistics for asking, and to some extent answering a simple question: 'How do they do it?' He looked at effective communicators, ones who really made a difference in therapy and business and asked 'What makes them such an effective communicator?'. Using the methods of transformational grammar he modelled these communicators and identified a set of principles and many specific techniques and them applied them to new situations effectively. So successfully in fact that he made a career out of constantly developing and then teaching these techniques for personal excellence. This appealed to me, there were rules that I could apply to help me get where I wanted and communicate in a way that I wanted, and needed to, to get things done. It also lead me into hypnosis and into becoming a sports hypnotherapist, but thats another (though related story).

Of course, the irony was, I realised, that it was all common sense and the guys around me who I respected as great communicators and who with honesty and integrity were doing well and making friends and (yes) influencing people, were just doing this naturally.

So I became good enough with Bandler's techniques to be able to teach his made up discipline (Neuro Linguistic Programming) and I absorbed the methods and rules until they were in my unconscious competance. I don't think about how I communicate anymore, I just do. Along the way I grew in my career and personal life and eventually left investment banking IT for consultancy and got involved in the sales, negotiation, persuasion and business management side as well as the pure value added technical consultancy. This is where I found my communication skills invaluable, and also where I found a lot of people who were just like I was - technically strong, but lacking the interpersonal skills to step up from technologist to consultant.

To help bridge this gap, I designed and delivered a set of training courses at my consultancy, aimed at both new and experienced consultants. Topics included general foundation skills, such as communication and influence, and negotiation, and then more specific skills such as requirements gathering, running meetings and giving presentations.

This book has developed from my own continued learnings whilst a project manager, technical architect, trainer and consultant and my experiences in delivering consultancy and communication skill training in various guises. It follows a simple principle, that *communication is key* and starts with a set of foundation chapters designed to grow your communication skills, partially taken from NLP and partially from general psychology and best practice. In the second part of the book I focus on specific skills that a consultant needs and shows best practice and how your skill as a communicator underlies this best practice.

The intention is that you will thoroughly cover the foundation material and then dip in to the later chapters to help you prepare for specific instances or tasks. If you need to prepare a presentation or get ready for an important meeting, everything you need is here. I also hope that you will enjoy reading this book and taking part in the many tasks and exercises that have been designed to take you forwards with unconscious competence to become someone with excellent consultancy skills.

These skills can not only have an impact on your career, they can have a massive positive impact on your life. They did on mine. I wish you the best. And please pass them on in any way you feel comfortable, as the more people who have access ways to share, communicate and negotiate then the more creative and complementary the world will be.

Adam
Surrey
UK

Contents

CONTENTS

CONTENTS

Part I
Fundamentals

Chapter 1

What is a Consultant?

1.1 If you want a consultant to tell you what time it is, you have to give him your watch

A shepherd was minding his sheep, and for that matter his own business, on the somerset levels when red sports car came around the corner at quite a rate. It pulled up with a screech and a man in a smart, probably tailored, suit jumped out.

'Hello' he said.

'Ar', nodded the shepherd

'Listen my man' he said, 'if I can guess how many sheep you have, will you give me one?'

'Alright then' said the shepherd, a man of few words, who probably had a particularly manky sheep in mind already

The man went back to his car, got out his computer and a set of survey equipment and started work. He studied google earth, created statistical analysis programs and after an hour of working he announced his result.

'You have 823 ewes, 3 rams and currently 657 lambs'

'Ar', said the shepherd. And he pottered off to the field and came back with a suitable animal 'here ee go, thisun be thine'.

He handed it over and man put the it on the back seat of his car. He was just about to get in and drive off when the shepherd said: "Hold on bud, if I can tell ee what job ee do, can I 'ave my sheep back?' It sounded like a fair deal, so the man agreed.

'Ee be a consultant'

He was correct, and the man, taken aback asked 'how did you know?'

'Well', said the shepherd, 'it were easy. You turned up unannounced, to solve a problem I didn't have, you gave me an answer that I already knew and you don't know diddly squat about my business. Now give me back my dog'

Every funny story comes with a grain of truth, it has to otherwise it wouldn't be funny. And there have been times where well known consultants and consultancies have performed a service exactly like this. I have seen it myself, junior consultants trundling along in a line through the trading floor, following the one senior consultant, writing down everything they see and then presenting it to the client as new knowledge. But these times are gone. Clients expect more for their money, and they will only engage consultants and consultancies where they see added value. This value can come in a number of ways:

Specialist knowledge and experience

The most usual justification for consultancy is to bring in knowledge that is not available in-house. And this is how those consultancy firms that specialise in a specific area or technology win business. Along with knowledge comes the more important experience. Consultants have often seen the same problems in a number of organisations and institutions and can usually solve problems or address issues much more quickly as a result. If you get the right consultant there is no voyage of discovery to the right answer, you are paying them because they already know it, and just need to apply it in your organisation. In many ways, you are buying the answer.

Flexible engagements

Consultancies are often used to provide short term specialist help or to provide manpower to projects at various stages. Permanent or even contract employees are usually not as flexible in terms of allocations on projects, and projects usually don't require the same people and the same amount of people throughout the project life-cycle. Consultancies can also provide the right resources at the right time in the project which is not possible with permanently contracted staff. There is clearly a risk to the consultancy and a cost of having people available to slot in and out of projects but some of this risk is accepted in the pursuit of profit and some is priced into the consultancy fees.

Delivery Responsibility

Consultants and consultancies are delivery focussed. Often paid by results they take responsibility for delivery governed by a set of conditions and a calculated risk around the fees and their ability to deliver.

Independence

Consultants and consultancy provide an independent service, one that sits outside of individual careers in and office politics in the host organisation. It is often said that consultancy are hired so that there is someone to hold accountable in the event of problems - i.e. you can always blame the consultant. This lets the manager off of the hook. Usually though, it doesn't come to this, since the consultant has no career or power agenda that intersects with the client and is often seen as non-threating (also often seen as a waste of time and money though, so be careful!!). This independence is useful and combined with skills of influence and organisation is a good way to get things done in an organisation that is stuck in a political rut.

Service oriented

This is a little contentious, but I strongly believe, as do many of my colleagues, that consultancy is the delivery if a service, not the delivery of people, and I carry this message with me when I meet clients, partners and other consultants. The bodyshop model is certainly profitable, but the profit is directly proportional to the number of bodies sold. This encourages consultancies to add people at a day rate to a project, often unnecessarily. Smaller specialist teams can often achieve the same results, and deliver a service to the client rather than just more staff. Of course the client needs to recognize this value and pay fees for it appropriately, and the mindset shift is that they pay fees for a service, or fees for results rather than for hours spent working. I will say more on this later.

Relationship

The consultancy service extends beyond the specific project and includes advice, account management and future support. The consultant/ client relationship develops before the engagement, is strengthened during the engagement and continues after the engagement. In fact, a number of my clients have become my personal friends over the years, but this is not necessary for business. A good strong mutually trusting professional relationship that develops over years of delivering good service and of being treated fairly. The best kind of consultancy relationship is one in which you become a trusted advisor, someone who can be called for advice or to discuss an issue, with an understanding that there is a line between this and a consultancy engagement. For developing business, for delivering a service and for enjoying your work, building relationships is essential.

A consultant is someone who delivers a consultancy service, its a simple as that. Consultants differ from contract staff because although both are often engaged as specialists the consultant delivers far more outside of the general specialist area. This is not to say that contract and permanent staff can't deliver a consultancy service, in fact the best ones do - making sure that that add value outside of their specific task and focussing on delivery and on becoming a trusted advisor. This in an excellent way to build a career, and quite apart form internal consultant roles such as architects and technology officers, almost anyone can act as if they were a consultant and benefit from the trust and relationships they build.

1.2 Consultancy as partnership

One tradition sees the consultant as a saviour, in which the client wants help and the consultant has the knowledge and experience to offer it. In this sort of consulting engagement the consultant has power over the client through the knowledge that he has, often knowing more about the clients business than the client himself - or at least claiming convincingly that he does!!

This is a fragile relationship that may net short term gain, but is only valid for as long as the client feels that the consultant has more knowledge than they do. Part of the engagement is based upon a pretense that the consultants really have something that the client can't get elsewhere and there is a lot of focus on presenting themselves as knowledgeable, powerful and competent rather than any tangible delivery. More problematic for the client there is no incentive for the consultant to develop the client in order that they eventually have their own skills for success.

An alternative is to see consultancy as the process of empowering the client through the creation and maintenance of a value-add partnership. In this model, the client and the consultant work together co-creatively towards a solution, learning together as they achieve their goal. In this approach the consultant is seen as trusted advisor, and facilitates the process of getting to the solution, but doesn't necessarily have all of the answers. Both the consultant and the client develop and this leads to a longstanding relationship and mutually profitable engagement.

Truly masterful consultants have the confidence to share knowledge openly and freely and work to develop a client centred partnership They know that their value to the client is in their capability to create an impetus for learning and transformation through the quality of their character . Working with a partner in the change or discovery processes the aim is to leave the client more capable that when they started, ensuring that they have ownership of the decision, output, process , resulting capability and deliverables, and that they are in the driving seat as much as possible. Ensuring that the client has freedom of choice, and all of the necessary information in order to make the decision that they need to make.

It may seem counter intuitive, but the best consultants ask questions rather than give answers. Making the client is ultimately responsible for the consulting outcomes has the effect of creating a sense of ownership. I wonder how many times consultancy engagements have resulted in rimes of documentation that has been left on the shelf after the consultants have left and never been opened. The outcome should be that the client feels compelled to action the recommendations when the consultant leaves, because the client has been bought in to the outcomes through being part of the process that identified and agreed them. To this end the clients needs and the clients uniqueness are paramount in the mind of the consultant. Cookie cutter approaches are not conducive to good client relationships and products and services need to be customised to meet the clients unique needs.

Fundamentally the partnership approach to consulting is based upon two simple premises:

- Client learning is at the core of the consulting activity

- The client is capable of solving its own problems and transforming itself

These premises have driven my approach to consultancy and I have found it to be both a personally rewarding and profitable approach. I have developed long term client relationships and friendships in my consultancy career. Recognizing that you don't have all of the answers, and realising that that is OK , in fact almost that it is better, is the first step on your way to becoming a masterful consultant. It is all about having the right approach and attitude.

1.3   The consulting mindset

Being a consultant means having a consultant's mindset, it is an attitude as well as a set of skills. This attitude comes with a confidence in your capability to lead the client in a process of discovery. Of course the client values your knowledge, and so should you, but the real value is in the successful way in which the consultant transfers this knowledge through a mutual learning process.

Our training and education system usually values knowledge and thinking over doing and there are standard ways of gaining information, such as researching or buying it (through reference materials or perhaps through consultancy). However clients can only gain knowledge by being part of the consultancy process, and what's more by being part of that process they then own that knowledge. This makes it much more likely that they will take actions based upon the knowledge, which in turn will make your consultancy intervention much more successful. And of course, ultimately will increase your status as trusted advisor so that you are called in to carry out more engagements.

A consultant develops the attitude and mindset necessary to become masterful when he realises that his role is the facilitator in the learning process. In order to do this well he needs skills that are rarely taught such as: building and maintaining relationships; communication; emotional intelligence and creativity. Some of the following would be considered necessary, but not sufficient, characteristics of a good consultant.

- Analytical ability

- Honesty

- The ability to understand the client's point of view

- Courage and a strength of conviction

- A commitment to learning - for yourself and the client

- Curiosity - ask questions first, then shoot later

- Brings their whole self into the consulting partnership

There is of course a threshold of knowledge in your field that is necessary to be a good consultant and credibility in the first instance comes with demonstrable domain knowledge. So a consultant must always be developing domain skills, but not at the expense of the client. This is easy to achieve for the most part as it is a happy accident that domain skills and experience grow as a result of each consulting engagement, although this should not be relied on as the exclusive method of development of domain skills and self study, reading, conferences and even trainings are all valuable ways of increasing knowledge.

A truly masterful consultant will comfortably admit what they don't know and spend time exploring issues with the client as opposed to swanning in and giving answers. They see consulting as a human process of which the consultant is but one part, and they focus not only on their piece of the puzzle but try to see it as part of a whole system. They are a guide, advisor and above all a partner in the discovery process.

Chapter 2

Foundations - Developing relationships

2.1 Building rapport

One of the key skills required not only as consultants but also in life in general is that of building strong rapport. This skill is central to all social interactions, and is is fundamental in negotiation, influence, sales and all aspects of communication. Many people can automatically gain rapport, in fact you do this all of the time with your friends, family and with people who you just 'seem to get on with' . There are always those whom you feel so comfortable with even after the first meeting. If you don't have rapport with your friends, family, partners or colleagues, you aren't going to get much done. If you don't have rapport with your client, colleagues and people in the organisations in which you work you aren't going to to be able to get much done.

This is why consultants, sales people and people who

want to do business together will do activities together such
as go out for lunch, dinner, a few drinks or to the grand prix.
It is not to butter up the client or to create one side of the
relationship, but rather to get to know them, and to build
a relationship with them. The more you know about them
and the more they know about you the more comfortable
you will be together. The more likely it is then that when it
comes to a consultancy engagement they will think of you
to partner with.

We like people who are like us. If you look around at a
party you will see people standing together chatting, leaning
towards each other, holding drinks in a similar way, laughing
simultaneously. These people are in rapport naturally. And
we tend to build rapport with people who have common
interests or are from a common background for example.

Rapport is a relationship between two or more people.
It is usually tacit, and arises spontaneously, but it can also
be built. In some situations it may not come naturally, and
so it must be constructed. There are a number of ways of
doing this, enough ways to fill books and bookshelves, but
the principles are simple. There is actually only one principle
and it is summed up in the following simple phrase - 'You
like people like you.'

Essentially this means that to build rapport, you have
to match the other person as much as possible. To really
build rapport with someone we need to match their language, physiology, experiences and thought processes. We
will begin with physiological matching.

The process of matching is straightforward; it is simply

14

the process of copying, or mirroring, the person that you want to build rapport with. As they move their left hand, you move your left, as they lean forward so do you, if they cross their legs so do you. Some of the things to look for are:

- Standing/sitting;

- Legs crossed;

- Angle of body;

- Nodding of the head;

- A twitch or tick (any mannerism);

- Wiggling of the foot.

You may think that copying someone is obvious and a little rude, and of course you should be subtle about it, but you only have to look around to find a group of people having a chat, in the office or at a party for example, to notice that those that seem to be subconsciously comfortable with each other are standing alike, and moving alike. Rapport building is a natural process, and all we are doing here is making that process explicit so that you can become excellent at communication; giving you skills that are essential for a consultant.

Of course, you don't have to do exactly the same as the person that you are building rapport with, you could choose to *cross-match*. In this process you match one action with a different one; as they move their right hand, you move

your left, or perhaps you move your foot; as they wiggle
their foot, you wiggle your finger. This process sets up a
link with their unconscious. It is particularly good when you
want to match a tick or twitch without seeming as if you
are being rude.

We can go one step further. More subtle, fine-grained
and effective matching, leading to deep rapport is done
through matching elements of physiology such as breathing, voice tone and speed and blinking.

Breathing - match your rate of breathing with that of your
client. Watch the rise and fall of their shoulders to
gauge their breathing rate (it often helps to be slightly
to the side of them to see the subtle movements in
their shoulders). Matching breathing can be done anywhere and is a very powerful and instinctively primor-
dial way of building rapport - notice how two people
asleep together breathe at the same rate. In fact if you
want to help your partner or your child go to sleep,
you can match their breathing as you drift off into
sleep yourself. Genie Laborde [2001] tells a story of
a client where she was asked to attend a negotiation
but was not allowed to speak. By matching breathing
only she was able to help to reduce tension between
her client and the manager that she was negotiation
with and create an atmosphere of mutual agreement.

Voice - match the rate and tone of speaking. If someone is
speaking fast, then speak fast to match them, and if
they are speaking slowly they will not appreciate it if

you try to race the conversation along. You may also match the tone of the voice, for instance whiny, soft, deep, harsh.

Blinking - match the rate of blinking. We all blink, all of the time, at a certain rate. As we get tired we keep our eyes closed in between each blink for longer. Matching the rate of blinking with your own blinking, or cross matching by moving a finger or foot at the same rate is a powerful way to build a connection.

> **Try this**
> Match someone. A great place to do this is in a queue or on a train or a bus. Pick someone and subtly begin to match parts of their physiology, the way they sit, the way they fidget and move. Once you are sure you have built rapport then start changing your physiology a little (sit up, or slouch). You will be surprised at how they follow you (if you have matched appropriately that is).

2.2 Pacing and leading

Once you have built rapport by matching, you will find that as you move, the person with whom you have built rapport will move with you - as rapport goes both ways. This is unconscious movement. You can then start leading. So if you want to encourage someone to follow your ideas, or line of thought, or even just follow you, first match them. Build rapport physically, and then as you see that they unconsciously start to match you, start leading. They will follow.

Have you ever tried to calm someone down who is angry by lowering the rate of your speaking and by being calm?

You may say something like 'calm down'. Doesn't this just make them worse? Before you lead you must pace, so first of all raise your voice and speak in an animated way, you can agree with them (more matching) and you can understand why they are angry (if appropriate) but do it at the rate and volume and with the movements that they are using. Once you have built rapport then you can start the process of leading; start slowing down your voice, and movements, become gradually calmer. They will then follow.

Next time you go into a shop or restaurant, match the person who serves you. Be enthusiastic if they are enthusiastic; be slow if they are slow. Smile. You'll be amazed at how accommodating they are, just because you have built rapport. Try this with your clients, when you go into a meeting start to match the person next to you, or the meeting chairman, notice how they start to follow your physiology, and begin to feel comfortable with you. And you with them.

The easiest way to match someone is to match her experiences. You must have come across people who are interested in the same things as you are, with whom there is instant rapport. This is not necessarily because you like the same things, but because you have experienced the same things. Walk into a room and say *isn't it cold outside'*. Notice that everyone will start nodding (as long as it is cold outside!!). You are immediately starting the process of building rapport.

As well as including content that can be metaphorical and induce mindset change, stories are a wonderful way of sharing experiences. Telling stories, then, is a great way of

sharing experiences that are common to a group and building rapport. Have you noticed how experienced managers,
salesmen and consultants will just chat to their clients or
peers, perhaps telling a story or two. Sometimes we just
relay stories about how we had trouble getting to work, or
how the weather on the weekend spoiled our cricket match.
These stories all serve to build a connection, to create report, to develop relationships.

The process of building rapport is simple and it is essential in the development of relationships as well as in the creation of an atmosphere or an environment that is conducive
to negotiation, questioning, training, presenting, running a
meeting and a variety of other tasks that a consultant would
perform as part of their daily work. It is simple but it does
take practice. And remember - *you don't need to be too
subtle.*

2.3   Representational systems

Physical matching is both a sign of rapport and a method
of creating rapport. We can extend this matching beyond
the physical by an understanding of how people represent,
store and think of things. We do not all think of things in
the same way, but when we do find someone who thinks like
us we are usually both surprised and pleased to find how
like us someone is. Its one of those 'Wow, I was thinking of
that too!' moments. Of course, without being able to mind
read it is difficult to know what someone else is thinking.
But there are some specific tools that we can use to help

us understand *how* someone thinks, what kind of thinker they are, and if we can match their thinking process then we are a long way towards building a strong relationship. Remember, *we like people who are like us.* We are going to make use of the idea of *Representation Systems.*

The notion of representation systems came out of the work of Bandler and Grinder (1977) and Bandler (1982). They are key ideas, central to the model that describes how communication works and essential in the process of building exquisite rapport. In this section we will explore very fine distinctions in the way that we represent things internally known as *modalities.* To get started, have a go at the following exercise.

How do you represent success?
Think back to a memory of one of the finest moments in your history a time when you shone, when you were extremely successful. Now pay attention to how you represent this inside. Make a picture inside your head of this time. Notice what you see, notice what you hear, notice how you feel. Can you smell or taste something too?
Write it down.

You probably haven't noticed until now but we store memories and experiences in our memory using all of our senses. Our primary modalities of taste, smell, touch, sight and hearing (not necessarily in this order), allow us to attach meaning to any experience real or imaginary, remembered or constructed. They also allow us to make comparisons between the way that we represent events, and the meanings we attach to it. For example the way that you represent failure and success will be different.

It is clear that we make representations of internal experiences in many different ways, and in ways that make sense to us. This perceptual organisation of experience refines and makes distinctions between internal resources. The value in knowing how things are represented and related is that resources (like confidence, power, concentration etc.) can be immediately accessed just by recalling the structure of that experience.

We can get to even finer distinctions which give us even more control of our representation processes.

2.3.1   Submodalities

Even more useful and explicit distinctions can be made. These are known as submodalities. These break down each of the internal representations into significant sub-distinctions. For example, when you look at your image of success is it colour or black and white, is it fuzzy or clear? In the film *Dead Poets Society*, Robin Williams plays an eccentric teacher who in one scene asks his pupils to climb on the desks in the classroom so that they can get a different perspective. He could have discussed the idea with them, but by asking the students to actively engage in the process he allowed them to access a whole new experience.

Our primary modalities match our senses directly - taste **(Gustatory)**, smell **(Olfactory)**, touch **(Kinaesthetic)**, sight **(Visual)**, and hearing **(Auditory)** - and allow us to attach meaning to any experience and make comparisons between different representations. It may sound strange, but you may see that once you experience this for yourself, by noticing finer and finer distinctions you begin to get a feeling for how you organise your own internal experiences. This is a valid model of the way that we make sense of the world; it allows us to think about how to alter the structure of our experiences by altering the structure of our representations.

For example we can divide the visual aspect of your experience into a number of sub-distinctions - for example between black and white and coloured, fuzzy or clear, still or moving images. These distinctions are known as submodalities, and it is these submodalities that allow us to make exquisitely fine changes, in just the right place to make the difference that makes the difference.

Let's give a simple and direct example of this. You may have a key presentation coming up, and one way of building confidence, personal presence and ensuring success is to prepare a run through of how the presentation will go. Most of us do this in our mind many times over, visualising ourselves completing it exquisitely. You can see yourself at the front of the room, speaking confidently, feeling good. But how much more of a valid experience do you think that you would have if you were to hear applause at the end of the presentation? And how specifically was the applause, was it quiet? Was the sound rich, loud, echoing, vibrating? Was there harmony, rhythm? What was the pitch, pace, timbre? Where was the sound coming from? These distinctions are the main auditory distinctions.

Coding representation systems
Go back through the text, go inside and make a representation of anything (pick something pleasant!!), think and write. Write down all of the sub-modality distinctions that you can think of in the three main systems: visual, auditory, and kinaesthetic. Use the following table:

Visual	Auditory	Kinaesthetic
Fuzzy - Focussed	Loud - Quiet	Warm - Cold
		Light - Heavy

2.4 Building rapport through language

We have seen how we can move towards rapport through physiological matching, but just think how much more profound that rapport could be if we were able to match the thought processes and representations of our clients and colleagues. Often, when you are in deep rapport with someone, a loved one, then you just seem to think alike. Have you ever found yourself saying, 'I was about to say that'? Sometimes the level of rapport is so strong that you know what each other are thinking, you are in tune. This depth of rapport is not only reserved for couples and close friends and can be achieved by matching at a different level.

Modalities and submodalities give us access to our internal representations, and amazingly we can notice the same distinctions in others through paying attention to their language. One way of thinking about language is as an externalisation of internal processes. Of course the process of externalisation passes through a number of filters, yet we are still able to identify what is going on internally in someone else just by paying attention. Just take a look at this list of visual words that we often use to explain or express things:

Coloured, vision, view, perspective, fuzzy, clouded, clear, detailed, wide-angle, See what I mean?

We can make similar lists for auditory:

Hear, sounds good; Don't like your tone; Rhythm; Volume; Are we singing the same tune?

And kinaesthetic:

Feel; Heavy; Light; Pressure; Running with it; Hold on; Handy; A bird in the hand; You get my drift?

Categorise each of the following sentences as visual, auditory or kinaesthetic

I can't seem to focus on the problem.
Something is stopping me moving on.
I can't really tune into that idea.
That caught me off balance.
I have got a blank on that.
That doesn't really resonate.

To build rapport, simply listen for the use of visual, auditory and kinaesthetic words in the language of the person that you are building rapport with, and feed back to them language that uses the same system. If I say 'You see what I mean ?' you can say 'Well, that's an interesting perspective.' Here are some other examples:

- 'I don't have a good feeling about this' - 'Yes, it leaves me cold too.'

- 'Here is my vision for the future' - 'It certainly is colourful.'

- 'Ok let's pump up the volume on this one' - 'Sounds great!'

Once you are aware of this, then you will begin to notice representation systems in people's language. In particular, many of the cliches that people choose are sensory-based and have a direct relationship to the ways in which they represent things internally. From your understanding of modalities you should easily be able to see how what you hear can give you a feel for the way in which someone thinks[1]. If they use mainly visual words, then they may be more visually oriented. The same goes for kinaesthetic and auditory. So to begin to build rapport, match their language, and so match their thoughts

---

Matching representational systems in language
Write a reply for each of these sentences that matches the modalities. For example:
Statement: *My view is that X is Y* - Reply: *I see your point*
You try:
I can't seem to focus in the problem
Something is stopping me moving on this
I can't really tune into that idea
That caught me off balance
I have got a blank on that
That doesn't really resonate

---

[1] read this sentence again - what do you notice?

One of the advantages of using language in this way is that it means that you can start the rapport building process over the telephone, or even in e-mail or in any other correspondence (in fact it is easier here, because you have a lot of time to think). This is particularly valuable with clients as you can begin to pace them as soon as they initiate a telephone conversation. Not only will they feel more comfortable with you, and more likely to come, but it also means that you have already begun one of the key processes in consultancy- building of a relationship. The consultancy relationship is based upon trust, and rapport is absolutely essential in building this trust. You will be amazed at how much more you can get done just using these simple techniques in all areas of your life. So start now, and let magic begin!!

Chapter 3

Exquisite Communication skills

3.1 The meaning of a communication is the response you get.

I once watched, and overheard, a sales manager giving a pep talk to one of his staff just before a key client meeting. This was the third meeting, and the one at which the sale was expected to be closed. The previous meetings had not gone as well as they might, but at least well enough to keep this salesman in the running. It was clear that his company was in the lead due to having completed previous good work and a competitive proposal. It was by no means, however, a done deal and the sales manager had had to bring the previous meetings back from the brink of disaster. events and was well behind. I can't exactly remember the pep talk word for word, but I was sufficiently struck by it to recall snippets. It went as follows:

'What is the matter with you? You're nervous aren't you? Don't think about how badly the last meetings went , because if you are as bad as that this time you aren't going to win. You want to win this one don't you?' (The student nodded.) 'You can't afford to fuck it up. This is yours to loose'

Well, the meeting was as terrible as the last one, and predictably the sales team were thrown out of the competition. It is clear that the language used by the sales manager didn't have the desired effect, you probably got an intuitive feeling for that. Let's analyse what he said, and look at why exactly it was that his language didn't work in the way he had hoped.

One reason was that the entire pep talk was predominantly negative. In order to think in the negative you have to first think in the positive. If you were asked not to think of a frog, you would probably have to think of a frog first in order to not think about it[1]. Try this. Don't think of a purple orange. What happens? We will all think of something, but not many of us will do anything other than think of a purple orange. Most of us will have thought of a purple orange first, and then not think about it. In general, our subconscious minds ignore the negative, and go straight to the positive. Remember when you were a kid? 'Don't feed the animals.' What is the first thing that you would do?

---

[1]eh? Perhaps you should read that again...

The second reason is that within the managers pep talk, there are a lot of embedded suggestions: You are nervous; you are bad; you aren't going to win . This is of course not the message that the manager wanted to put across. Nonetheless, it is there, embedded in his speech.

So the question is, how do you avoid making this mistake and make sure that the message that you do want to put across is in fact the one you do put across? This is a key point in communication. Fundamentally:

We, the communicator, are responsible for the communication.

If someone doesn't get it, its not their fault - it is ours and we must communicate more clearly. This is a very empowering realisation, because it puts you in control of the communication.

Jaques Derrida, a poststructuralist writer, was one of the first to articulate this notion clearly [Derrida, 1980]; He identified that *author* of a text (written or spoken) and the *reader* (listener) as having roles of creator and interpreter respectively. He made it clear that what the author intends to communicate is not necessarily what the reader takes from the communication.

Communication is not absolute. What does this mean for us? Simply it means that we have to be careful how we communicate and we need to make sure that our message is understood. How do we know that it is? That is the hard bit. We can watch and see how the reader responds, and we can ask 'was that clear' (usually if the answer is yes it pays to ask more detailed questions to make sure). Richard

Bandler and John Grinder expressed idea clearly this in one of the fundamental principles of NLP:

The meaning of a communication is the response you get

3.2 Using effective language

We communicate through talking and writing every day, all day. And we are all acutely aware of the impact words can have on us, how they can make us feel. One or two words can turn us from a calm rational human being to a screaming banshee (a good couple of words for this is 'just calm down' , which usually has the opposite effect to that which was intended). The words that we choose, the way in which we choose to use them, and even the order in which we choose to place them can have a profound impact on our ability to get the message across. Fortunately there has been a good deal of study of the most effective ways good communicators use language, and through a study of salespeople, managers, therapists, public speakers and negotiators a set of basic language skills suitable for all types of communication have emerged. In the following sections we will outline these basic skills, giving you all of the tools you need to get your message across effectively. We start with the idea of suggestion.

3.2.1 Positive language and Suggestions

We are giving suggestions to people all around us, and to ourselves all of the time, There are two types of suggestions: direct suggestions and indirect suggestions. Indirect suggestions are found in areas such as advertising, training and negotiating as well as in a form of hypnosis known as *permissive hypnosis*. They are also found all over the place, in our conversations (and in our pep talks!!). You will be able to hear them, see them and read them everywhere when you start paying attention to what you are reading and hearing. The previous sentence is an example of indirect suggestion. Not so subtle examples are 'Buy now, pay later' and 'Smoking kills'.

Suggestions appeal directly to the subconscious in an unambiguous and unconstrained way. This fact is utilsed by advertisers on billboards and television all of the time. Giving useful, good, positive messages is an important skill for managers and for anyone who wants to drive an idea forwards, and to achieve buy-in from participants.

No-one likes to hear bad news. People like people who are positive. Its a well worn cliche but I once had a manager who told me 'bring solutions not problems' and he was right. Managers, and clients do not usually have time to investigate the minute of a problem and come up with creative ways problems. They are so busy they have only time to make decisions, and they rely on you - the trusted advisor - to bring them the options and to suggest the best approach, which essentially they endorse. You, as a consultant, need to bring them the right answer, stated positively and suggest the right approach. That means not saying 'we can't', 'we don't' but instead saying:

'The problem is that the database team have no

> *time, what we need to do is re-prioritise project*
> *A now and focus them on project B'.*

This is a suggestion, and it has all of the characteristics that give it a very good chance of being accepted.

Suggestions must be positive - .'What we need to do is...'

Suggestions must be progressive and may be continuous - in other words they must refer to the present and future rather than the past - ' re-prioritise project A now and focus them on project B'

Suggestions must be phrased simply and clearly - the subconscious can't be bothered with sentences that are too complicated.

So for example, it is better to say 'The way forward is to get everyone in a room' instead of 'No one is talking'.

3.2.2 Using your voice to help create a positive response

There is one tool that is invaluable to us: our voice. The difference between a relaxing, calm, guiding voice and an annoying, irritating, grating voice is that one is nasal and the other starts from deep down in the stomach. Imagine what it would be like for a child to be read a bedtime story in a whiney, nasal voice. We are pretty confident that our children would not find that a suitable preparation for getting ready to go to sleep!! What about a nasal salesman?

CHAPTER 3. EXQUISITE COMMUNICATION SKILLS

Would you buy your goods from someone with a voice like a strimmer? (Maybe if you were buying a strimmer I suppose.) You need to develop your skills in creating the right tone of voice, have a go at the following exercise.

Try This
Take a novel, children's book or newspaper article and practice reading it in different tones of voice and different types of expression. In particular pick a tone that is relaxed and comes from the stomach as opposed to one that comes through your nose. Your aim should be that you could read any section of any book to someone in a way that would make them feel calm.
Record yourself reading. Does it sound relaxing or calm? If not, then keep trying, remember read from your stomach.

You should be starting to sound different, and you should be starting to notice the different tonality that various people have around you, and the difference this makes in their ability to communicate. Take a senior manager that you know who is clearly very senior, ask yourself what it is about the way they communicate that makes them senior. Think about the way that they stand, hold themselves and speak. You will generally find that powerful people have a voice that comes from the stomach. This gives them a presence, gravitas. Take Churchill for example or Barack Obama. Ask yourself what makes them so compelling, so powerful?

You don't have to sound like Churchill though to be an effective communicator. In fact it is important to be flexible, to match your communication with the people and the message. For example it is important that when you say words like *learn*, you say them in a way that encourages learning. Or *delivery* that you say it is a way that gives confidence in your ability to deliver, or an order to deliver to someone else. You must be confident, and say words meaningfully and with enthusiasm. Now, don't get me wrong, I am not suggesting 'over the top' enthusiasm, more gentle enthusiasm. With learning, for example, we want you to be able to recreate a positive, curious, feeling and experience for your training delegates or meeting attendees, and you can start to do that by correct use of your voice.

It is particularly important when making suggestions that you use the correct tone of voice. If you pay attention to those around you or in the media who seem to be able to get things done, seem to have a commanding tone, you will notice three things. First they speak from their stomach and their tone is low (deep); second they use direct, deliberate and slowly delivered commands, and more subtly (and most importantly) they inflect downwards as they say the command. This means that at the end of their sentence/command, they drop their voice lower. If you raise the tone of your voice at the end of a sentence, this generally indicates that the sentence is a question, but if you lower the tone it becomes a command.

Try saying the following sentences, first by raising the tone on the last word and then by lowering it.

- Take your time

- Don't forget to have a good time

- Buy now, pay later

- Have a nice sleep

If you have children, a tip in story reading is to drop your tonality at the end of each sentence that you read, surprisingly you will find that they become more and more tired throughout the story, especially if you read it in a slow, low deliberate voice, and yawn occasionally.

To make a suggestion more powerful, and to indicate that it is really a command, it is important to emphasise the commands by dropping the tone of your voice on the key words.

- It would be good if you just sit and **listen to me**

- Don't **go to seep** just yet

- Although this room isn't a **scratch** on the previous training room. **your** still going to be able to learn; but nobody really **knows** how the room will impact that! (say the last sentence around a group of people and wait to see how many of them scratch their noses!!)

3.2.3   Positive affirmation

We all enjoy praise, and it is nice when we are told that we are doing things right. By focusing on the positive and always rewarding or acknowledging good behaviour, we find that good behaviour increases. This is a basic premise of behaviorism, a psychological approach which underlies many methodologies of training and teaching based on the punishment and reward system. Behaviourists (such as B.F. Skinner and S. Pavlov) were able to generate appropriate responses in rats and pigeons by rewarding them when they got something right (through food usually) and punishing them as they got something wrong (often with pain). This generates a feeling of going away from the bad behaviour and towards the good behaviour. In this way Skinner was able to train a Pigeon to fly a missile [2]!!

Knowing what we know about positive language and the subconscious, we know that it is not appropriate to point out what not to do, as this only brings the undesired action to mind. In setting powerful goals we can use the idea of moving away from a behaviour that is not desired (as long as we express that positively), but in the case of the language of influence we clearly need to focus on the positive and reward good behaviour. Just doing this simple thing has very strong, positive consequences.

We can do this simply, and unobtrusively. When you give a suggestion or instruction to someone, and they respond by doing what it is that you have asked, you can say 'That's right', or 'Excellent' to affirm the good behaviour.

> *Take a quick look at the plan.. (wait for response)... That's right. You can see that we have covered all points... excellent*

---

[2]During the second world war Skinner demonstrated the possibility of having a Pigeon guide a missile to its destination through pecking at the centre of a target, fortunately (for us and the Pigeon) it was deemed to risky a solution and was never implemented

Try this simple technique of positive affirmation at work, with your friends and family. You will be amazed at the results.

3.2.4   Truisms

You want to learn how to communicate with your clients better, and you want to ensure that you are able to influence your clients in the right direction. You know that the route to being an excellent consultant lies in improving your consultancy skills, and so you need to learn some of the tools and tips in this book.

One of the most prevalent mechanisms for convincing you to do something is the truism. Truisms occur naturally in sales, business, and negotiation and it is only relatively recently that their use has been formally identified. What are they?

A truism is a statement that you make or a question that you ask whose answer you know already, and the answer is usually *Yes*. The use of this type of language is an elegant and efficient way of pacing and leading just through the language you use. Truisms give a link between the experience that the person that you are communicating are having having and the experience that they will be will be having next, leading them from one state to the next. For example:

> *You are sitting there, listening to me, as you begin to think about how to accelerate the project*

It is undisputed that you are sitting there (as long as you are) and that you are listening to me, but you may not be aware that you are about to think about accelerating the project. In fact you may not be doing that until the embedded command 'begin to think...' is given.

Truisms divide into two main classes: internal and external. External truisms are those that are externally observable or verifiable such as 'It's chilly in here', 'You can hear the music.' Internal truisms are truisms that can only be verified by the person that you are communicated with, by going inside themselves such as, 'I am sure you are curious about...' and, 'you are clearly aware of certain factors.'

Take for example this statement:

> You can see the project plan in front of you, the work packages are clearly marked, I am sure that you are wondering how easy it will be to deliver .

Here we have a number of external truisms - you can see the project plan the work packages are clearly marked - then internal truisms - you are wondering... Notice too the way in which the statement paces (where you are - what you can see) and then leads (where you are going - how easy it is to deliver).

Truisms
Imagine that you are going into a meeting to convince your manager that the new project schedule should be supported with extra budget and resources.Write down 5 truisms that you can use that that are EXTERNAL - statements that can be verified. Example: You can see the project plan.

> Now write down 5 truisms that are INTERNAL - statements that cannot be externally verified. Example: You are thinking.

3.2.5   Yes Sets

This leads us to the over-used, but highly effective, persuasion technique of *yes sets*. If you want someone to agree with you on anything they have to be in a frame of mind where agreement is possible, and natural. You know, I am sure, all too well the frustration of getting to a point in a discussion where it is logical and reasonable to get an agreement, but impossible because the other person just won't budge. Are they being difficult? Not really, they just aren't in the habit of agreeing with you. In order to gain a 'yes' on an idea or to gain a positive response you need to get the person that you want to convince in the habit of agreeing with you. This is a common approach used in advertising, where things that we can't possibly disagree with, truisms, are used to develop this habit before the killer advertising hook is applied. This approach is called the 'Yes set' technique.

There is a simple rule for yes sets, and following it has a powerful effect. You will recognise this rule in action in advertising and you will see it in direct sales techniques. You can even use it on your boss if you want a raise. Why don't you try? The rule is: If you make three statements that someone else can agree with easily, the fourth statement can be a command or a direct suggestion which has a very high chance of being followed. For example, do you recognise this pattern?

1.You want a car that is safe. (don't you?)	*1st Truism*
2.You want a car that is economical to run. (don't you?)	*1st Truism*
3.You want a car that is comfortable to drive. (don't you?	*1st Truism*
You want the Pico 23ZXR	*COMMAND*

We will look at lots of examples of yes sets during the course of this book, and in particular in relation to influence and presentation skills. I have already used one or two in this chapter - why don't you go back and see if you can find them? Yes sets are quite subtle if used correctly, and you can find them all over the place.

> **Yes Sets**
> Take the truisms from the last example that you did, and use them to write a yes set that will convince your manager to adopt the new project schedule

3.2.6   Indirect language - Double binds

There is one further, exceedingly powerful, language pattern that is used all the time to influence, and is invaluable in persuasion. It is often used and taught as a course technique for covert persuasion to sales and in particular telesales staff and is easily recognisable. It is not recommended as a way of forcing someone to a decision, however as a subtle approach to influence it is a valuable tool. In this section we will look at it purely as a mechanism, you will see how we can use it subtly and with consideration in later chapters.

The technique is the double bind. Consider the following conversation:

'Hello, I would like to talk to you about our double glazing product.'

'I don't really need any new windows right now.'

'I understand that, and I also know that sooner or later you'll be thinking of upgrading.'

'Well, yes that's true.'

'Shall I pop round on Thursday or Friday and chat to you about what we have on offer?'

'Er... Thursday would be best'

Did you notice the particularly sneaky way that the salesman lead this conversation? In two places he offered the customer a choice without actually offering any choice at all. Let's explain what we mean here.

Sooner or later you will be thinking of doing it - The choice here is sooner, or late, the assumption of course is that she WILL be thinking of doing it. This gains an agreement with the customer and the salesman then proceeds to securing an appointment.

...I pop round on Thursday or Friday? - the client hasn't actually said that they want the salesman to call, but the salesman gives them the choice of two days and they pick one. The assumption then in the salesman's language is that he already has an appointment, and he gives the customer a choice, but not of whether he will be invited around, rather of when!!

These are double binds. A double bind is a statement or question that gives the illusion of choice. In each of the cases above there is a choice presented, but the choice that is presented is irrelevant in terms of the real intent of the statement.

Here are some more examples of double binds:

a) *You can sign now, or as I talk*
b) *I don't know how soon you will do that*
c) *You can choose to accept it now, or later*
d) *Do you want to get dressed before, or after you have had your breakfast?*

In each of these cases, there is an underlying intension or presupposition.
a) You will sign
b) You will do it
c) You will accept it
d) You will get dressed

Double binds
Write down double binds for the following situations
Getting a pay rise
Getting a meeting with your manager
Closing a sale on a car

We are of course not suggesting that you would use any of these techniques to secure an appointment in the same was as our imaginary salesman, but used in a sensitive and appropriate way double binds can assist in inducing change, creating new opportunities and to influence decision making.

3.3   Using the right tools at the right time

I remember many times when I have used a knife to undo a screw. You know what I mean, when you are trying to change a fuse quickly you pick something out of the cutlery draw. The knife isn't quite right but it sort of does the job, usually taking longer and often ruining the screw and the knife in the process.

As you can probably tell I am not very good at DIY. When I moved into my new house I found a superfluous pipe going nowhere, sticking out of the floorboards in one of the bedrooms. Every day when I passed it I thought to myself that I really must deal with it, but I never did get around to it. Until one day when I decided that this day was the day that I would address myself to the problem. So I got my hacksaw, and knelt down and started sawing the pipe off near the floor. It was when I had cut through the first edge that I realised my mistake as water started spurting out at quite a rate. Apparently although the pipe was indeed superfluous there had been something attached to it at some point and it was blocked off but still on the main heating circuit. Well that's what the plumber said.

You have responsibility for using your tools of communication in the right circumstances to solve the right problems. Your toolbox now consists of a number of useful items - rapport, matching, mirroring, suggestions, truisms, double binds - all of which can be used to help you communicate more effectively, more efficiently and more exquisitely. But just like my knife, they are not appropriate for all tasks, and just like my hacksaw you have to be careful how you apply them.

One of the questions that always comes up when I run training is the appropriateness of such tools. Are they not manipulative, do they not give you an unfair advantage? But all of these tools are already being used, consciously or unconsciously, by excellent communicators all over the world. People that we look up to for their ability to get things done, or create resolution or build relationships at the top level are all using these tools, probably without knowing. They are what we call 'natural communicators'. I guess that you are reading this book because you feel the need to improve the skills that make you a great consultant, and those skills are partially a set of tools for communication.

Now that you are in possession of many of the same set of powerful tools that the best communicators have, you also have a responsibility, a responsibility to use the tools with integrity. Just as I can't blame the hacksaw for flooding my house you can't blame the yes set for selling you a car that you don't want, or making you buy a bottle of coke. Think carefully before you apply tools of influence, and make sure that you are comfortable with the outcome that you are creating. Ensure it is an outcome for mutual gain. Sometimes it is better to go to the toolbox and get the screwdriver rather than use the knife, and it is sometimes best to think carefully before getting out the hacksaw!!

Part II

Consultancy Skills

Chapter 4

Influence and Persuasion

It is impossible to persuade someone to do something if they really don't want to do it. You can sometimes force them, bully them or trick them but doing this has short term gains and will be detrimental to any future relationships or dealings with them. This is the buyers remorse problem.

Consultants need to be exquisite influencers. In fact most of the job of the consultant is to encourage people, or teams or organisations to move in a certain direction. This can be a short process, such as encouraging someone to meet you to talk about an issue, or arranging a sales call, or it can be a long process for example encouraging the Board of a company to accept your proposals for business process change. Influence is the art of establishing movement towards a solution or outcome through the creation of shared common goals. Influential people understand this, and know how to use the tools of communication to their advantage to create an environment in which they can find a suitable set of common goals and generate momentum for a solution.

Influence, persuasion and negotiation all seem to be considered to be the same thing, the same process. In fact many books and trainers seem to use them as synonyms of each other. I don't disagree, but then again neither do I agree!! Of course, they are all connected, influential people need to have the power to persuade, and good negotiators need the capability to influence. For the sake of structuring the discussion and separating out some tools and processes we see persuasion and influence as two sides of the same coin, we can point to six principles of influence, and a process of persuasion. Negotiation on the other hand is a specific process that we will deal with in a different chapter. Lets make it clear though that when you want to influence, you will use all of the tools, skills techniques and approaches at your disposal. Remember, *if something doesn't work, try something else.*

4.1 Influence

We have already looked at some of the specific tools of influence, such as simple language patterns and *yes sets*, in the earlier chapters. Having excellent rapport and superb communication skills are the fundamentals of being influential. Look around you at people who you consider to have influence, or who are able to convince, influence or persuade easily. Most of these people will have naturally good communication skills. They may unconsciously utilise yes sets, double binds or other tools and patterns. It is these exquisite communicators who have been modelled in order to understand what makes them so good at what they do, and from whom the patterns of success that we have covered have been drawn.

These skills are at the level of personal interaction, and are skills that can be used during the process of influencing, at the time of working towards an outcome or gaining influence. However it has been noted that there are a number of factors that create the momentum for influence. These were first enumerated by and are very well illustrated by Cialdini [2007] in his excellent book, and have formed the basis of sales and persuasion books and training ever since.

4.1.1 Cialdini's principles of influence

Reciprocity

Acts of kindness are generally repaid, sometimes manifold. People are usually more willing to do something for someone who has already done something for them, and in fact are often compelled to do so even if they perhaps would not have before. This is one of the main approaches in sales, although many sales people are not honest with themselves about using this device. Salespeople and Directors often entertain clients, take them to lunch, football games, for coffee, give them gifts, and sometimes they give them knowledge or information that is useful. This creates a momentum around reciprocity, as well as of course giving many opportunities for growing trust, confidence and rapport (which is usually what sales people will say that they are doing).

Consistency

We don't usually like to break commitments. People are more willing to comply or move in a direction if they see it as consistent with an earlier commitment that they have made. For example if, at the end of a meeting, you were to ask for agreement to discuss a point further at a subsequent meeting in the next dew days, and you got a nod from everyone around the table (which you would usually get from everyone if you get it from the first one or two - see Social proof below) then when you call up the participants to schedule the next meeting they will usually agree or comply, because they have made a commitment to do so. Often, double binds are good ways of ensuring a tacit and inescapable commitment.

Social Proof

We are more likely to do something if other people do it. We should never underestimate the power of group mentality. We often go along with the crowd. This is because of two main reasons: the first is that we don't need to think about it too much, it must be safe or the right thing to do as everyone else is doing it (there is after all safety in numbers and a desire to fit in); the second is that we don't want to be seen to do something outside of the rest of the group (we are told - don't rock the boat). Successful stage hypnosis is based upon social proof. Stage hypnotists rely on the fact that many people who behave as if they are hypnotised in a show only do so because they are on stage in front of 100's of people and feel pressure being the only one who isn't hypnotised. It also helps that afterwards they can blame the hypnotist for whatever actions they performed on stage. I lived for a while in Greece in the 1990's and I noticed that every Greek teenager was indistinguishable, wearing timberland sand colored boots and puffy jackets with ducks on, even on the hottest days. I guess its true then than no-one ever got fired for buying IBM!!

Liking

We are more likely to agree with someone we know and like. It is easier to agree with someone if you like them. Amway and other pyramid sales organisations know this, which is why thier entire business model is to have you sell to your friends and family. Client entertainment is as much about rapport and relationships, as it is reciprocity. And in fact some of my clients over the years have become really good friends. As friends they are careful to separate work from friendship but they trust and like me as a friend and so will take my opinion on board. We like people who are like us, and rapport building is one of the key skills of the influencer.

Authority

We are more likely to follow someone who appears to have authority. The classic case here, which is explored by Cialdini in depth, is the case of the experiment designed to understand the limit that a human would go to in causing pain to another human before stopping. The basic idea was that a subject (experimenter) would be given controls that were supposed to give an electric shock to another subject, and was to be instructed by the doctor (complete with white coat) to increase the shock every time the recipient answered a question wrong. The results were unexpected. The experimenter continued increasing the level of shock despite the clear indications of severe discomfort from the experimetee and severe distress to the experimentor, increasing it to dangerous levels on the command of the Doctor. Fortunately the experimentee was only an actor, but it proved a very strong and valid point about following orders. A strong example of this was the defence used by Nazi war criminals after the second world war, that they carried out crimes under orders[1]. If you have authority, or apparent authority, then you have influence.

Scarcity

We are more likely to covet or pay more for something if it is rare, or is not going to be available for much longer. Shops use this gambit often as is evidenced by slogans such as 'Limited time offer' and 'Last one left'. In the commercial world we will often caveat prices or deals with statement about the duration that the deal is valid. A consultant I know once was able to achieve a pretty solid salary increase by letting his boss know that he had a job offer, with a better salary, that he needed to decide on within the next

---

[1] This is known as the Nuremberg defence, but was unsuccessful as the prosecution argued that they still had a moral choice if they did not agree with the order

three days. In this case he was the scarce commodity. It always amazes me though that someone would pay a million dollars for a stamp that originally cost only one penny. I guess that is the ultimate in putting a value on scarcity.

Try this
As you go about your daily life, you are constantly bombarded with media, advertising, news and information, and you are the recipient of many attempts to influence you in to buying, trying, discarding, reusing, going, eating, not eating and various other things that someone else (usually the Government or business) wants you to do. These organisations know about the principles of influence, and use them openly. Now that you are aware of them you should recognise easily. Write down two examples of each of Cialdini's principles of influence as you find them being applied to you through media such as the TV, newspapers, advertising and the Internet

---

It is easy to relate to these principles of influence, by understanding how we have been influenced over the years by people and organisations using these mechanisms. We can also easily see how these principles can be applied in sales, and in places where we may need, as consultants, to get a decision or agreement. In whole or in part these mechanisms of influence are valuable additions to our toolkit, but we should be careful how we apply them.

4.2   Persuasion

For me, buying a car is a relatively unpleasant experience. Its a lot of money to part with and I see a car as a necessity not a luxury. I have no clue whatsoever of the various mechanical and electrical features that make any given car any more or less valuable and as far as I am concerned as long as it starts every morning, gets me where I want to go, is warm and has a reasonable stereo then I'm happy. The last time I bought a car this complete lack of interest in any features seemed to annoy most car salesmen, as after telling me about the latest gizmo all they got was a blank, disinterested stare. Of course, people are different. A friend of mine seems to buy a new car every year, and each time proudly explains to me that some new gizmo is an absolute necessity and well worth the upgrade.

The last time I bought a car, I tried perhaps five showrooms (I only buy second hand because of the depreciation issue) and each time the salesman annoyed me within 5 minutes. Their approach was to ask me what my budget was, show me three cars under budget, then give me a feature dump before I had a chance to say what I really wanted, and finally to start negotiating on price before I had decided to buy. They usually told me that it was the last one (*Scarcity*), or that two or three people were looking at it seriously (*Social proof*), they all told me that they would give me a good deal on my part exchange (*Reciprocity*) and one even said that he was 'telling [me] to buy it' (*Authority*). I wasn't going to buy, even if it was a great car, as I didn't feel part of the process. It was as if they were making decision for me. I am what is known as a *polarity responder* (essentially if you *tell* me to do something, I am very likely to do the opposite) so I don't respond well to a hard sell.

The approach from the salesperson where I eventually bought my car from was different. This salesman seemed to want to spend time with what sort of thing I was looking for, what my feelings were about how I would use the car. He listened (or so it seemed), and I actually quite liked him. After a while he took me out to the forecourt and showed me around as few cars. Some I discarded as too cheap or too expensive (which helped him on the budget I guess). He asked me to sit in each one and feel how comfortable they were (or not). He asked me if I had a CD in my car, and I went to get it. We tried it in all of the car stereos with me sitting at the wheel. He asked me to imagine myself driving to work, sitting in traffic in each car, did I feel comfortable, relaxed? He asked. I narrowed it down to two and we then began to discuss a deal. I picked the one with the more solid driving feel and he threw in a new stereo. I was, and am still happy with the car as it was my choice (or at least my perception is that it was my choice) and when I want to change it I am going back to that salesman, whichever dealership he may be working at.

> **Try this**
> Think about the two different approaches to selling illustrated here. Which method would you prefer to be used with you, and which do you think would be more successful. Which approach would you tend to use.
> Now think about the second approach more carefully, what was the process used to persuade me to buy the car, what were the key differences?

Why did I buy from the last salesman? What made

him persuasive? Simply it is because he built a degree of rapport, listened and understood my requirements and then helped me understand how one of the cars matched those requirements. I liked him, he paced me, and by the end I trusted him, and he lead me. The key point that this salesman understood was how to persuade or convince me. He realised that I did not care about alloy wheels or a long list of features, I wanted to know how the car felt, and how the stereo sounded and how I would feel while driving it. You will notice that he used simple devices, like playing *my* CD and having me imagine how the car would feel while I was driving it along a busy road to help me check with my internal representations of what I wanted.

We often come across this problem as consultants. The client has asked us to present some findings and recommendations to the board, and we prepare a meeting pack and presentation deck and send it to him for review. We may have used the latest presentation techniques and we may have filled the presentation and pack with all sorts of statistics and detail, but the client isn't happy. Usually its because although the conclusions are as they expect, the story isn't told in the way that they want. It doesn't match their internal representation of what they imagined when they tasked you with the job of preparing the material and presentation. This is easy to fix, you merely ask - 'what is it that you are looking for?'; 'How can we change this to match what you would think would be most effective?' But it is better to do this questioning in advance, and to work in conjunction with the client to produce the material to their expectations.

Specifically, we can use our knowledge of the way that people represent things internally to persuade them in elegant and effective ways. Knowing what they feel, hear, and see when they imagine something can help us. I am sure that you have had a time in the past when someone has said that for example 'It seems to me that you like a bit of luxury' or something similar, and that exactly matches your thoughts. In these cases you usually immediately feel a connection with the person and are more open to further discussion. After all, if they know what you want already (are they mind readers?) then they must be the right person to help you get it. They are a kindred spirit!! As artful influencers we are not mind readers, but if we listen carefully to the words that people choose we can identify the way in which they represent things and can use that responsibly in our persuasion approach.

- I don't really *see* myself sitting in that one.

- I thought it was *clear*?

- Thats out of *synch* with my idea.

- Lets *grab* this while we can.

You see my point? More details of this internal process (known as submodality distinctions) and what to look for are given in the first section of this book and are clearly described in Bandler [2008]. Of course this process also starts to build up the Yes sets that are often used to start the habit of gaining agreement (See Chapter 2). This begins to create a matching and a pacing, and eventually a leading, and here everything starts to come together.

Overriding the art of exquisite persuasion and influence is a framework of pacing and leading. Essentially that is all you need to do. Pace your client, enter into their world, their view of things, walk a mile in their moccasins. Match their breathing, their movements, their internal representation systems, and as soon as you feel that you are pacing them deeply and unconsciously then you can start to lead them. Make sure that what you lead them to, makes sense for them and fits into their view of what they want and who they are (that way you avoid buyer's remorse). This process is very well illustrated in Bandler Bandler and LaValle [1996].

4.3   Decision making strategies

People have very consistent decision making strategies. Think back to the last time you made a decision. See what you saw, hear what you hear and feel what you felt at the time you made a decision. Fully associate with the experience of making the decision. What mental process did you go through? Many people will look at the possible results of a decision, having done or bought something, and see themselves in the future having made the decision. They will think about how that looks, feels, sounds and then will check the way they feel about that. If it feels good then they will decide to buy, choose or whatever. If it doesn't they will choose the opposite. This decision strategy is very common, and sales people have keyed in to it 'Can't you see that TV in your lounge, it feels good to be watching such a clear picture doesn't it?' These salespeople are right... and they are wrong.

They are right because the principle of keying in to peoples decision making strategies is correct, they are wrong because not everyone has the same strategy. We all apply a feedback loop of some sort (well, most of us - some of us just make decisions without any real strategy at all). We will consider an number of options, often talking to ourselves about them or considering different scenarios. Some of us go round a loop many times - we look at an item, we check with our internal scenario or self-talk, we decide if it sounds, looks, feels right and apply whatever decision criteria, and if its a 'no' or a 'maybe' we may loop again with another scenario or another option. At some point we will make a choice, based upon one or more of the three sensory criteria - it looks, feels or sounds right.

You can map it out, by drawing V (for visual), A (Auditory) , K (Kinesthetic) on a piece of paper and connecting them in your own feedback loop. Here is mine.

Understanding how people make decisions and they keying in to that strategy is a key influencing skill.

I have never drunk so much coffee as I have being a consultant. I once had to get a steering committee to agree to move forward on the purchase of some software. It seemed a simple thing at the time but what I didn't realise until I started was that out of the 5 members of the committee,

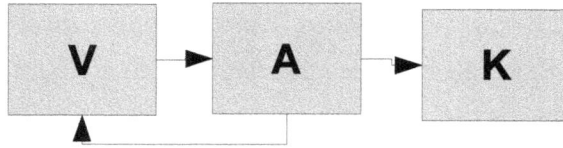

Figure 4.1 – My buying strategy - 'I look at the item, then I say to myself...., eventually it feels like the right thing to buy and so..'

two were indifferent, one (my boss) was already a yes and the other two had a different agenda. I found this out because I did the usual trick of syndicating the decision before the meeting. The idea here is to meet everyone individually and to check their level of buy-in. If they aren't really bought in, then you use all of your powers of influence and persuasion to achieve a consensus. This way you get no surprises at the meeting. But sometimes, you have your work cut out, as I did.

One of the two who would say no, I found out, had some previous grudge against my boss and would say no out of spite. The other had a previous relationship with the a competing software vendor. I met him first, for coffee. In our discussions I found out that he had a personal relationship with the competitor vendors sales manager, and that he really valued this level of engagement. He hadn't even met the people involved with the product that we were suggesting. I also found out that he liked football (which I really don't). During our meeting I took care to build rapport, and trust through pacing. I listened to the way in which the senior manager expressed himself when talking about the product.

In particular I noted that he wanted to be comfortable that it was backed up by a strong company with quality values.I made a call to the sales manager of the software product and suggested that he take this senior manager out to lunch, perhaps organise a tour around the company HQ and later on suggest a trip to the football.

I met the two managers who were indifferent, separately, for coffee. In both cases they said that they didn't care about the choice of software, they just wanted it to work. One said that he just wanted confidence in the product, and I asked him how I could give him confidence. He said that if he felt he could trust my opinion, that would be enough. The other manager said that he would see how it went and would probably just go along with the group. During both meetings, I took the time to build up rapport, to listen and to clarify in my mind the primary ways in which each manager represented ideas and made decisions.

How to deal with my boss's adversary? It was clear that he was working to another agenda, and that the software was not really of importance to him. I decided to meet him (for coffee!!) and to build rapport at the very least, as that would help in the meeting. In the meeting I asked him about his functional requirements, which were all very detailed, geared towards the competitors product but mostly irrelevant in relation to the business requirements. As we chatted I noticed that he kept talking about having a gut feeling about things, and taking hold of the issue - he was clearly very kinesthetically oriented, and I wondered how that could be useful in influencing him. He did state his main objection to the vendor of choice was that it was a small company, not one of the big three. During the meeting I matched him, his breathing, his physical posturing and his language, and by the end of the conversation we were chatting about cricket (one of his interests, that I happen to know a bit about) and had generally good rapport.

> **Try this**
> Look back through the description of the scenario here, and think about how you would run the meeting. What would you say, to whom and in what way? How would you influence the decision?

On the meeting day I arrived first and made sure everyone had coffee (again!!). I chatted with each participant as they arrived. When my boss's adversary arrived (fashionably late) I continued our conversation about cricket for a while, and my boss came over to join the conversation (and grab a coffee), I joined him in the conversation. My boss had played village cricket in his younger days, and could be found on the boundary with a Pimms on warm summer evenings. I left them chatting. I then pulled the group together ensuring I engaged everyone. We chatted about the weather, and the difficulties in traveling to work that morning, and the fact that since it was winter it was already dark. We look at how to run a meeting and how to do a good presentation later in the book so I won't go over this here, but the way in which the meeting was set up was a key part of the process.

When the meeting started I decided to bring the group together and start the habit of agreement before stating the objective.

Thank you all for coming, and for taking the time to be part of this process. I know you are all busy and its been a long day, we don't often get such a prestigious group together, and while I know that you all agree that it is important to spend some time on this we are here to make a decision about the best software for the job. I'm sure that with the information on the table this will be a straightforward decision, and we will only spend the time that we need, to come to an agreement.

Having created rapport with the group (and to some extent within the group) I set up the meeting with some yes sets I presented the information. I made sure to inoculate the group against the objection that the company was small by pointing out that it had a string balance sheet, lots of customers and was agile. 'We want the company to be responsive to our needs, not like some large monolith with endless bureaucracy'. I then gave a list of requirements and a discussion of how the candidate software matched them. It was a good match, a slam dunk. well, almost...

This company is small and agile, with a good balance sheet. The product matches all of our requirements, and the price is good. I am confident that it will work well and help us achieve our business objectives. Are you all happy to agree to go forwards to a commercial negotiation?

My boss agreed, the manager who had had the tour and felt that he now knew the company agreed. Both managers who just wanted it to work, agreed. Would social validation be sufficient to pull along the difficult manager? I said 'we have to make this decision today in order to benefit from the limited offer price', trying a scarcity approach. And then I remembered that he was kinesthetically oriented.

> *This is not the first time you have made a decision like this, in fact if you think back I would hazard a guess that in the last six months you have made a choices that, at the time you may have had some unanswered points, but you went with your gut reaction and now feel like it was exactly the right thing to have done. In this case its an easy decision for you, as we know that the software works, we have a good feeling about the vendor and we are confident that it will meet our objectives.*

My boss then added 'come on George, this is a full toss, lets just knock it for six and move on'. It was a slam dunk.

Chapter 5

Negotiation

Negotiation is the process that two parties go through to establish a set of common goals or outcomes that both parties are happy with. It is very important for you to understand this kind of negotiation not as a game with winners and losers but as a framework for getting to the right answer and for getting things done. We often get this wrong, with disastrous consequences. I once went to buy a car. I saw the car I liked, it was priced at £6200, and I only had £5500. I did my research and saw that in part exchange I would get about £5200 for it. So I went in to the car showroom and found the salesman and offered him £5300 for the car. He asked me to sit down and said that he was sorry, he couldn't move from the price on the windscreen, or his boss would 'have his guts for garters'. I said 'Ok, £5500, that's my final offer' (and it really was). He said, 'sorry £6200 or no deal'. I walked out of the showroom.

My friend came to pick me up to go out to the pub three weeks later, and he was driving the car I had wanted. He said he bought it from the nice salesman at the garage for £5600, a good deal he thought. Apparently the sales guy had wanted to shift it form the forecourt, it had been there for three months already.

It is important to realise that *negotiation is a process*, although not necessarily a linear one. There are two stages in this process, first and most important is preparation then, once prepared there is the actual negotiation. Here we view negotiation as a way of dovetailing outcomes, that is, finding a set of outcomes that give each party what they want at some level. The best negotiations are those in which everyone feels like they have won, and the best negotiators are those who can follow a process to get to a solution without becoming personally involved in the process. Of course, there are those who see negotiation as a game, and apply a number of gambits to see if they can achieve some advantage. We will look at some of them here, but the overriding principle is that if you are clear on your objectives, you understand your limitations and you maintain integrity you will walk away with a good solution.

5.1   Be prepared

This will be a theme throughout this book. A good consultant, like a boy scout, is always prepared. Preparation is extremely important in everything that we do, and part of the skill in consultancy is knowing what to prepare (and how to efficiently use your time in doing so [1]). If you enter a negotiation without being prepared you will not be effective, in fact you will almost certainly come away with a less favorable outcome. So what are the components of preparation that you need?

Understand the outcomes clearly

You absolutely must insist on objective criteria, whether you are negotiating on behalf of another party or for yourself. It is extremely important to understand the purpose of the negotiation, to be clear about what you and your opposite number are trying to achieve. You should take time to specify the full set of outcomes that you want from the negotiation. This can be in terms of price, or scope and can also include other objectives such as repeat business, or steps towards promotion for example.

It is equally important to understand the outcomes on the other side of the table. If you don't know them you will have to make a best guess based upon your knowledge of the situation. Try walking in their shoes for a while to see where you would be setting your outcomes if you were on that side of the table. If you do this you will clearly be able to see where the outcome mismatches are, and what the sticking points of the negotiation will be. This will help you prepare.

A common approach to the specification of outcomes is

---

[1]Although we do not cover time management here, it is a key skill of any effective person. If you need help in this area I recommend taking a look at the time management section of Covey [1989]

through the well known SMART criteria

SMART outcomes are:

- **S**pecific - This distinguishes aims from outcomes. For example you might *aim* to address an issue, and the *outcome* you require would be to gain agreement on it.

- **M**easurable - There is no point in setting an outcome without clear criteria that allow you to see whether you have achieved it or not. As an example you might look to get within 15% of your target.

- **A**chievable - It goes without saying that you should set outcomes that are within the limit of your capability to achieve. It makes no sense for example, in negotiating a pay rise, to set your outcome at the pay level of a Director when you are two levels below.

- **R**ealistic - Going hand in hand with the Achievable criteria, realistic goals are those that are actually achievable. In the context of a negotiation don't expect a systems integrator to deliver a complete booking system from scratch in two weeks.

- **T**imely - Timelines turn aims into outcomes. Outcomes are immediate, or at least have a time component. aims don't. It is key in negotiation, and in all goal setting exercises, to state by when an outcome should be achieved,

CHAPTER 5. NEGOTIATION

So a good SMART outcome for a negotiation on the scope of a project is: to include everything necessary to deliver to a specified set of requirements within a specified time period and with a defined number of resources (or budget).

An alternative, that I find personally more appropriate, specifically in the context of negotiation, is the concept of a well-formed outcome. As a general principle well-formed outcomes satisfy the following criteria:

- Are stated in the positive, and are specific

- Specify the outcome in terms of what you will see, hear and feel when you have achieved it.

- Identify the evidence that will convince you that you have achieved it

- Consider the context that this outcome will occur in.

- Consider the purpose and consequences of the outcome. Why do you want it, what will it do for you and what will it do for others.

- Identify the resources that you need in order to get from where you are now, to where you want to go.

We can take SMART outcomes and pass them through the well-formed criteria to help us think about what we want to achieve in a way that opens up possibilities for creativity in negotiation. Lets take the example above: *to include*

*everything necessary to deliver to a specified set of require-
ments within a specified time period and with a defined
number of resources (or budget).* It is certainly positive and
states what we want to achieve, not what we want to avoid,
which starts us off in the right direction. Outcomes such as
'I don't want to end up with too short a timescale' focus on
a negative outcome, which is unhelpful, backward looking
and quite frankly depressing. Unfortunately by focussing in
what you don't want you often forget what you do want.

Assuming we have a definition of the requirements, time
and resources then this outcome is specific enough (it is
SMART after all). The next two criteria are covered by
asking the questions 'how will I know that it is done?' and
'what will it look like when it is done?'. These help in
planning and also set the criteria for success. It is extremely
important to know what the criteria for success are up front,
otherwise you will never get sign-off that the project has
been delivered, that the outcome has been achieved. In
the case of our SMART outcome we will know that we have
achieved it when the customer has signed off on the delivery,
and that we are on time, in budget. We will see a happy
customer and a working system - which is a good image to
have.

Questions about why you want the outcome are usually very revealing. It may be that when you really ask the
question of yourself, or of your boss or of the other negotiators you find out that you are about to enter discussions
about something that no one is really sure about. Before
you are prepared to be creative around a point, and move

on a position, you need to understand why you are holding that position and what you really want to achieve. It is important to think through the consequences of achieving an objective in the mid and long term. Something that looks goon now may not look so good in 6 months time. As you consider your SMART objective, you need to think if it really is the right thing to commit to. For example agreeing to deliver a project now may prevent you being able to deliver other projects, or give you significant concentration risk at a single client.

I almost wrote 'it goes without saying' that you must make sure that you have the resources you need to achieve the outcome, but then I realised that the full set of resources are not obvious. By resource we mean at the very least financial, staff and personal resources. Negotiating to ensure that you have budget to complete the project is one thing, but you must have the skill, the time and the character to deliver, sometimes under difficult circumstances.

So having specified and checked your desired negotiation outcomes, you are in a strong position to enter the discussion knowing where you are aiming. If you can do the same for your opposite number that will help you to understand where they are coming from and help you plan your approach. A key part of the planning is knowing what alternatives are open to you in the event that you are unable to agree - your BATNA.

BATNA

There is no 'minimum position', only a best alternative to a negotiated agreement (BATNA). The better a negotiator's BATNA, the greater their power around the negotiating table. A BATNA is not the *bottom line* that reflects the worst possible acceptable outcome that is often seen as a hard-stop of some negotiations. Such a position, while useful and sometimes unavoidable (especially around budgetary constraints - although in the corporate world even these are often movable) creates inflexibility and prevents creativity around possible solutions outside of the fundamentals of the problem.

Buying things on e-bay is a good way to test your negotiation skills. More often than not, early on in the process you can have a conversation with the seller and negotiate some deal that prevents an actual auction taking place. I was recently browsing on e-bay and I noticed a nice guitar that seemed reasonably priced at £110, the postage and packing was billed at £20. I didn't really need a new guitar, as I had one similar, but I did think that at a good price it would make a great spare. I thought that the value of the guitar was around £100, and I just about had that available, so I contacted the seller and offered him £75 for the guitar. His wife emailed me back and said that he would not accept less than £90. She said that this was his *minimum position.* Understanding that he valued the guitar, and would not accept less than £90, ever, I offered him £100 for the guitar if he would throw in the postage and packing for free. We had a deal.

This is a simple example, but it illustrates a number of points. In particular here it illustrates how, since I didn't have a minimum position I could be creative in terms of my offer, and it illustrates that since he did have a minimum position (and he told me what it was) that I was able to use that to my advantage. It also illustrates that value of knowledge about whatever it is that you are negotiating on, and the value of working with people on getting a solution rather than battling them to get the best deal for yourself.

Minimum positions are important to prevent the negotiator accepting an unfavorable position. However the same can be achieved with more flexibility and grace through putting in place a plan of action which would be enacted in the event that an agreement has not been reached. The negotiator is aware of an option outside of the negotiation that is better than the proposed unfavorable position. This creates a position of strength and allows the negotiator to step away from a negotiation if it looks like it is going to become unfavorable. Sometimes the BATNA is as simple as not needing to come to an agreement (I didn't really need the guitar) and sometimes it is something outside of the negotiation, not know to the other negotiator, that is a good alternative.

As consultants we sometimes have to pitch for work, and in most cases when the proposal has been submitted there is some negotiation on price or scope, or both, before the work can be signed off. Usually a small price reduction[2] or

---

[2]Actually I don't recommend price reduction at all, although some-

a reduction in scope (which is the preferred approach) but sometimes the reduction required means that it is impossible to complete the work in the time, or price required. How you handle this depends on your BATNA. If you choose not to do the work, what is your alternative? Perhaps you have another more profitable engagement, or perhaps you can spend the time developing additional business or software to sell? If you have these in your back pocket then you will not be forced to cut prices to an untenable level and dilute your brand. It is a good strategy to always have a BATNA whenever you go in to a negotiation.

Find out as much as you can about the other party

Tsun Tsu is purported to have said something along the lines of 'Keep your friends close and your enemies closer'. This is good advice that has been followed for centuries, although in the case of negotiation the people with whom you are negotiating should certainly not be seen as your enemies. A good general knows as much about the plans, character, movements and strengths of their opposite number as they can, as well as having a full understanding of their own strengths and capabilities [van Creveld, 1985]. As you enter a negotiation you will want to have a full understanding of the other side as possible in order that you can direct the negotiation process to a suitable conclusion. You will want to know:

times it is unfortunately necessary, I'll discuss this later in the chapter.

- What they hope to get out of the negotiation - their desired negotiation outcomes.

- What their minimum position or BATNA is. This is key, as you will know how far you can push them in the negotiation before they will walk away or break. By contrast, you should never give away your BATNA, or minimum position.

- Any Achilles heels - weak points, misinformation, or something that will change their emotional state.

- The level of decision making power the negotiation team has - the more they have the more chance there is of achieving a resolution at a single meeting.

- And as much as you can about the negotiators themselves, what makes them tick, what they like to do in their spare time and similar. This all assists in the rapport building process.

Part of this information can be gleaned prior to the meeting through web searches, and telephone calls to colleagues who might know the negotiators, and perhaps a courtesy call to the negotiators secretary - they are often extremely good sources of information, but you will need your best influencing and negotiation skills.

The rest of the information must be ascertained during the negotiation. One of the key learnings that I had about finding out information is that in general, if you ask people, they will tell you. If you want to know the opposite parties desired outcomes form a negotiation, just ask them. They will tell you, and quite right too, otherwise you don't know where you are aiming.

Negotiation proceeds from positions of strength, and knowledge is power. Whilst finding out as much as you can about the other parties you should never give away any information about your position, or yourself. Of course, you can share unimportant information in the rapport building process through the use of universal truisms for example (see chapter 2) but it is key to ensure that you do not provide anything that is potential leverage, unless you want to as part of the game of give and take as the negotiation progresses.

5.2 Let's negotiate

Remember, the aim of a negotiation is to come away having achieved some resolution on a point that is beneficial to you. You will only achieve this if you can find a solution that is also beneficial for the other side. It may not be the objective that you had at the beginning of the negotiation, but through the process of negotiating and building up a relationship with the other side you can develop an outcome that suits both sides.

In the delivery of a fixed price project there is usually an agreed change procedure to ensure that project scope creep that is the responsibility of the client is chargeable. This concept while ostensibly simple is fraught with danger, as the sticky point is always who is responsible for the scope creep. In one case, a consultancy had billed a client for additional work that the client believed was only necessary because the consultancy had under delivered, and I was involved in the negotiation that was to decide who had responsibility and what should be paid, if anything.

Things hadn't gone well, and the client was irate having not expected any additional charges and not having budget available. We knew that they had a mechanism for getting more if it could be justified, but we also knew that it would present personal difficulties for the client project manager if he were to have to admit that project creep was essentially his responsibility. We also knew that we had underestimated would have had difficulty delivering to the original timescales, and that these additional things that had come up from the client had helped us by pushing out the project end date.

The discussion started badly, the client was clearly defensive and pushed back strongly saying that they believed that the delays were due to the consultancy and that therefore should be at our cost. We, of course, had stated the opposite. On a matter of principle the sales team felt that we should charge for the work and should stick to our position. To me, this rang warning bells. The relationship with the client was good, but not that good, and we expected (were promised) much more business in the next few months. I didn't want to jeopardize that on the basis of a position. I asked the sales team what their objective was, and it was clear that they wanted to ensure that they retained and profited from the client in the future. I helped them see that it was in their interest to focus on long term gains rather than short term. However the principle that they should be able to raise project changes and expect to be appropriately remunerated for them should be strongly established.

This was a tricky situation. In general there is no pre-scribed way in which a negotiation should proceed, and in fact like great battles planning is only useful until they start. The following points then should help you get through the negotiation and come out with a valuable outcome, or at least to know when and how to fall back on your BATNA. They are in no particular order, except that the first - build rapport - should be a constant.

Build rapport

Here you need to apply all of your skills to build rapport and relationships quickly with individuals and with the whole group, that will assist in coming to a resolution. The aim is to create a general feeling around the table that everyone in the room is working together to find a solution. Remember *we like people like us*, and we like to agree with people who we like. Sometimes negotiators start out very aloof, and often aggressive, just wanting to get down to business, this happens very often in formal negotiations such as those that involve lawyers. If this is the protocol, then you should ad-here to it (otherwise you will break rapport) but use covert rapport building skills, such as matching and mirroring pos-ture, representation systems and language. Otherwise you can also be more overt, taking time to chat before proceedings start making use of the knowledge that you have about the other parties. Perhaps they like golf, or football or you notice from their Panda like rings around their eyes that they have just been skiing!

Negotiators are people

The negotiation process is a decidedly interpersonal endeavor. Negotiations can be stressful, they take their toll on the people in negotiations and they test and strain relationships. Negotiation is not always a pleasant experience, and negotiator emotions get mixed up with the negotiation process. Remembering that both sides are going through the same trials and tribulations and difficulties, and respecting the efforts that both sides are making is important. This mutual respect helps create an environment and impetus for resolution. On the other hand, negotiators often look for *hot buttons* which they can press to create emotional responses which cloud reason and judgement and which they can use to their advantage, I don't recommend this, but be prepared to deal with it by remaining calm, rational and increasing your efforts to build and create rapport. They won't do this if you have good rapport.

Separate the people the process

Sometimes things will get a little tough, and discussions may even get heated. In many negotiations the negotiators are working on behalf of someone else or some entity, in others they are directly negotiating on something that effects them personally.   In both cases however it helps immensely to separate the negotiation process from the people and from their (and your) personal investment in the outcome. The idea, ultimately, is for both sides to work together to come up with a solution rather than seeing the negotiation as a battle.

If everyone has done their homework, they will know what their outcomes are, and what their BATNA is, they will be clear and usually realistic. The negotiation then is a process of coming up with a solution that meets both sides expectations. It has nothing to do with who is doing the negotiation or what their personal involvement is. Sometimes it helps to step back and view the process as apart form the people.

Focus on interests and not positions

A common approach to negotiation is taken from a practice in market and trading where both sides establish a position and then through a process of haggling end up with some middle price or ground. Setting out a position this strongly can be detrimental to the process as it tends to obscure what people really hope to gain from the negotiation, the underlying interests of each party. This idea is fully explored in, and is one of the main principles of *the* negotiation reference 'Getting to Yes' [Fisher and Ury, 1981] .

Dovetail outcomes

This is the real meat of the negotiation pudding, as it is the outcome of the negotiation that is the purpose for engaging in the process in the first place. Each party needs to come away from the negotiation without buyers remorse and to achieve this win-win situation you need to work together to invent options for mutual gain. These options must address your interests, and the interests of the other party. Sometimes it is very difficult to come up with anything, but once you chunk up to higher levels of abstraction you can often find a meeting point from which to build.

Respond to feedback

During the negotiation you need to be aware of how everyone around the table is responding. Pay attention to what they say and also what they don't say. Look for any physical signs that they are loosing interest, or changing emotional state. If they say 'that doesn't work for me' look to see how congruent that statement is with their true state. Listen to their tone of voice, sometimes how they say something won't match what they are saying, and pay attention to the redness in their face and whether or not they are fidgeting, indifferent or animated. People give a lot away.

It is not enough just to notice. You must take account of the covert and overt feedback you are getting and decide how to respond to it. Some of the valid responses would be: do nothing; change behavior; offer alternatives; changing tack. You must decide how to act on the feedback that you receive, it is a powerful way to grow rapport and make a difference to the negotiation process. It gives you choices, and remember, *choice is better than no choice.*

Be creative

We often will get stuck during a negotiation. Each side cannot move from a position and there seems to be no meeting of minds. This is a time to chunk up, to look for alternatives, to state objectives again in a different way and work from them, and to come up with ideas that can move the process on. In a word, its time to be creative.

The law of requisite variety [Bandler, 1977] states that *the most flexible element in a system will be the controlling element.* This means that the more adaptable and flexible you are the more you are likely to become the strongest player. This is the case in all areas of work and play, and it is clear that the best business, political and war leaders all exhibit incredible flexibility. Flexibility and creativity go hand in hand, you have to come up with ideas and approaches that you are prepared to try, to explore to adopt. You cannot stick to a starting position, inflexibly, and expect to find a resolution. So when stuck, come up with ideas that work, that achieve both sides objectives and serve both interests, and be prepared to reshape the negotiation, your approach and the outcome to find resolution.

Despite all of this it is not always possible to achieve a resolution.

It's OK to stop negotiations

If things are not working out, if you just can't seem to get to a resolution then as long as you have your BATNA in place you can feel free to agree not to agree at this time and cease negotiations. This does not have to be final, but it does give you an opportunity to think and discuss further options in a less pressurised context and also to refer to someone else perhaps more senior.

Referring to authority is useful device to be able to apply, even if it is not necessary. It is perfectly acceptable to say that you can't decide on a specific point, that you will have to ask the board. This gives time and also demonstrates to the other side that what they are asking is outside that which would be considered normally reasonable. Also it is a good way of saying No, eventually, without stretching your own relationships with the other side. It's a normal technique in sales, how many times have you asked for a 10% discount and got the response 'I don't know, I'll have to ask my boss', after which the sales guy disappears into an office, comes back and offers you 5% which you accept? Most times its the secretary, the accountant or no one in the office and if you were to hear the conversation it would probably go like this: 'that guy out there asked for a 10% discount, I told him I would have to talk to the boss, I'm gonna go back in a while and say the most that the boss could do was 5%, I bet he takes it'.

It is often a good idea to take time out of the negotiation when stuck on a single point just to think, or, if you are in a team, discuss the options and next move. This is called *going to the balcony* in negotiation circles, and it has a benefit for you that it allows you to step outside of the negotiation context and process and take time to think. It also doesn't prevent resolution that day, creates space to create more options and also creates some psychological tension and impetus for the other side who will be wondering what you are saying and thinking and trying to second guess an prepare responses.

As I have stressed, negotiation is a joint process, which moves towards dovetailed outcomes and shared resolution. Sometimes though it isn't possible to achieve this initially and taking time out is a good way for both sides to pause, think and come back refreshed for a new phase.

In the case of the fixed price project, I decided to focus the discussion not on whose fault it was, nor how much should be charged, but on the proper mechanism for raising changes and ensuring that they are agreed and responsibility assigned. We discussed the criteria for accepting changes. I stated that we needed to understand, for the future, how to do this. The client moved in to an explanation mode, and during the discussion we were able to build a bit of rapport. I said that out objective was to ensure that we all understood the process, not to focus on specifics. We all agreed that we wanted to work together. I then suggested that we look at the reasons for the current project delay in respect of the criteria that we had just discussed, which we did. During this discussion it became clear that a couple of the reasons for delay were actually attributable to the client.

He then agreed a split in fault and a split in fees. He was happy and paid less. We were happy that we had covered costs and made the client aware that we would not accept delays without payment. Win-Win.

During this process the client changed emotional state from irate and defensive to collaborative and positive. Part of the reason for this was in the quality of rapport that was built, and part of it was because the focus of discussion was chunked up a level to a point where some agreement could first be reached, and reframing the discussion on price as assistance into the exploration into the reasons for delay. All of the key points of negotiation came in to play and ultimately we ended up with a good resolution.

5.3 Commercial Negotiation

The basic principles of negotiation and influence are the same whether you are trying for a pay rise, working out a way forward on a disagreement with your partner or trying to buy, or sell, a car. However in the commercial context you may come across certain behaviors and it is useful to be able to recognise, counteract and in some cases apply them. In commerce, negotiation is often seen as a game, and as such professional negotiators will use a selection of gambits to try to get the upper hand. Additionally there is the notion of price, which is the key outcome, and it helps to understand how to set the price that you open with and the price that you will be happy with.

Working towards a fair price

It is a relatively simple idea, you know your costs, you know your margin and so you set your price, and as long as the buyer pays that price you will be happy. However, if you can get more than you hoped you will be better off, and of course you will be prepared to cut your margin to make sure you walk away with the business. If you are the buyer, you will know what you want to pay and you will know a fair price (and they may not be the same). You will want to get the best price you can, and there is obviously a price at which you would be prepared to go somewhere else. Somewhere between these two positions is a price that can be agreed on.

First of all I never negotiate on price. Secondly I always start pricing negotiations[3] with a universal statement that 'everyone is entitled to make a profit'. After all it is in the interests of the buyer that you remain solvent, and happy to support them in whatever way they need around the product or service they have bought. What would be the point of squeezing a second hand car salesroom to loss making deals, they are bound to cut corners on a pre delivery service and they may go bankrupt, leaving you in trouble if your car has problems during the warranty period. In consultancy you get what you pay for, and so if customers cut fees we have to provide lower cost, hence less experienced, resources with potentially serious impacts to the projects. Its false economy. But then again there is always a tendency to

---

[3]It is well known that *All generalisations are wrong*!!

over-egg the pudding.

The aim of any negotiation is to ensure that there is a resolution and that everyone feels good when they walk out of the negotiation room. Win-Win. In negotiations on price we ensure this by working out in advance the price range in which we think that there will be an agreement, and then using our negotiation skills to get as near the top end (seller) or bottom end (buyer) as we can. As an example, lets work out an area of agreement in this scenario.

Imagine you are selling a development project for 500 man days for £500K. Your margin is 20% (which is low by most consultancy standards, its just easy to work with as a number). Your minimum then is £400K , but your boss would fire you if you sold the project at cost, and has stated that you must make at least 10%or no deal. Your range then is £450K-£500K. You also know that the buyer could deliver this project using his own resources for a cost of £350K, but that he can't start immediately like you. You also know that he has had other quotes from the market that are little lower than your original quote, and you guess £480K and you also guess on principle that he will not pay your original asking price, as he has to show that he has added value to the process too. Thus his range would be £350K to £480K. Your ranges overlap at £450K to £480K. This is the range in which if you can agree a price you will both be happy.

The aim is to make this as near £480K as you can. And it makes sense to set a target as near that as possible, as a rule of thumb, you would set your agreement target at 1/4 of the distance from your lower limit to there upper limit. In our case at about £473K. Negotiation then proceeds from an opening position, towards the target. Of course you must start higher than the target to play the game, and usual advice is to start 25% of the range above the upper zone limit, in our case £487K.

Any movement from this starting price should be in small slices. We all have a tendency to want to find resolution quickly, and to try to shortcut the process of getting to an agreed price by moving in large chunks. Whether we give a large or small slice we are still showing willing and taking part in the negotiation process.

Closing the gap

On the way towards agreement there will be a gap between the two parties. In most commercial, and other, negotiations this gap is closed by each side offering concessions until a target it met. These concessions need not be financial and it important to remember that the final solution is a package of things, price being only one of the elements. For example you may be looking to buy a washing machine, and in the package may be free delivery, warranty, some washing powder and you may even get a discount voucher on any purchase from the shop within 6 months. Some of these may be valuable to you, and some won't but as a package it may make sense.

As you close the gap you may have to give concessions, on price or on the package. And you may also want to ask for concessions. There are a few simple rules of concessions that you may find useful.

- Ask for concessions, don't wait for them to ask you

- Always flinch at any requests, shaking your head is often enough, even if you accept later

- Remember that its a complete package, not just the price

- Give away things that are not valuable to you, but are valuable to them

- If you accept a concession, ensure that you make the conditions of that acceptance clear

There is an important rule about negotiation on price. *don't!* If the other party really can't afford your proposal reduce price by reducing value - never reduce price and keep the same value. We will discuss this point in more detail when we look at methods in later chapters but the principle is a simple one. Make sure that when you create your proposal you have a variety of different priced options, this means that the other party will then be able to pick the option that they can afford rather than ask for a lower price on the only option. Car manufacturers do this well, offering different versions of the same car with different features at different price points.

Last minute objections

Think of the archetypal plumber who always sucks in his breath through his teeth when he looks at your boiler, just before he shakes his head and says 'it doesn't look good'. His gambit here is inoculation. He is essentially setting out the idea that it will be a high price so that when he provides you a high, but not outrageous, price you are already in the mindset to accept it. Our plumber is not expecting last minute objections to the price because he has pre-empted it and dealt with it before it even arose.

The best way of dealing with last minute objections is *don't*! Do some pre-work to understand what they might be and inoculate against them. For example you might say *'I know that you might be thinking that this car is overpowered, but.... you always need extra power to get you out of an emergency situation, don't you?'*. Do you see how this works? The trick is to know what the objection may be first, and this takes some thinking, and some effort. It is certainly worth it.

If you do find yourself facing an objection that you haven't thought of then you need to take the objection as a new request or an additional factor and go back to the phase of the negotiation in which you put all aspects on the table. I would always say how surprised (possibly upset) I am to have this last minute unexpected change, but I would be prepared to make an effort to changing the shape of the offer to include this new objection. Sometimes this means inventing new options.

If you hit deadlock, where no agreement seems to be possible then its important to keep talking, keep referring to the higher level outcomes and back to the issues that you are stuck on. If you must give more in order to move forwards, only do so conditionally 'we can reduce the price but only for the first three months, or if you allow us marketing opportunities'. If you do your work right, you should never get to this point. Remember if you don't get to a resolution, then both sides lose, which does not satisfy the purpose of the negotiation as the best outcome of a negotiation is when both sides win. It may be time to stop the negotiation, and come back later or ultimately though, referring to your BATNA you can make the final decision to walk away for good if appropriate.

Let's hope it doesn't come to that.

5.4   Summary of negotiation tips

It is hard to remember all of the things you need to do when in the throws of a negotiation. The following is a list of top tips, that distills the main points in this chapter and will help you as you prepare for your next negotiation. Negotiation is a serious business, but you can have fun while doing it, so go ahead and enjoy the process.

- Understand the outcomes clearly

- You absolutely insist on objective criteria

- There is no 'minimum position' , only a best alternative to a negotiated agreement (BATNA)

- Find out as much as you can about the other party

- Separate people from positions and process

- Negotiators are people

- Dovetail outcomes - invent options for mutual gain

- Build and maintain rapport

- Respond to feedback

- Be creative

- Its ok to stop negotiations

- Make sure that you are negotiating with the decision maker.

- Understand your target price

- Inoculate against objections early

Chapter 6

Running a meeting

I used to be in meetings constantly, back to back. Some days I would have a whole day of meetings with no time in between, no time for lunch, or indeed for any abloutions!! By the end of a day like this I would be exhausted and have achieved little. This is not a useful use of anyone's time.

Now I have a new world order. I don't attend meetings unless they have an objective, a bounded timescale and an agenda. This way a lot more gets done, and I get my life back. Now when the people around me book meetings, even a key client, I always ask for the meeting objective and if there isn't one I suggest that we postpone the meeting until there is. It helps focus and ensures that I have more time to do useful things.

It sounds simple. But even when you get into a meeting you still have to make the time useful. Meetings are not opportunities for a rest (even though some people seem to take them to be!!) they are opportunities to get something done, to achieve something. This chapter shows you how to structure and manage a meeting to get to the meeting objective. It doesn't matter if you are meeting with an individual by the photocopier or you are running a board meeting, the approach is the same. The only difference is the money at stake - it's very costly to have a board meeting that doesn't achieve anything.

6.1   It's all in the preparation

If you want to achieve something from the meeting, make sure you prepare. If you don't prepare you reduce the chance of a successful outcome, and if you don't know what you want to achieve form the meeting, don't have it. You have to ask yourself seriously what the purpose of the meeting is.

Meetings can have one of two purposes:

Information - Both to give and to receive. Examples of this would be requirements meetings (including brainstorming and similar activities), scope meetings, project updates, dissemination meetings or information gathering about future projects ideas etc.

Decision and agreement - Simply these are meetings with the right people in them to make decisions, steps towards decisions or gain consensus on a point.

'Meeting up' with someone is not a meeting unless it has one of the two purposes above. It is a valuable rapport building activity, but has the capability to waste a lot of time. Meetings are expensive. As we have discussed, building rapport is essential to doing your job well, and coffees, business lunches and after work drinks all contribute to this, but if you look closely whenever you meet someone in a work context, even for a 'quick catch-up' you should be thinking of it in terms of information gathering or decision making. This way we use our time profitably, and our time is valuable.

Large or small, the key to a successful meeting is framing it well. This means thinking carefully about the following four aspects:

The Outcome frame

This is what the meeting is all about. We must ask ourselves what we want to achieve and what are the **real** meeting objectives? if the answer is that you don't know, *then don't run the meeting*. I mean it, and I can't stress it enough (as you can probably tell). Once you know your objectives use all of the tools at your disposal to state them clearly, well formed and SMART (see chapter 3). Then, make sure that you understand what you need to do in order to achieve these outcomes. You should also check that the other meeting participants will support the purpose of the meeting, and will support the proposed outcomes. You can do this through the process of syndication.

Syndication is a common way to ensure success of a meeting, and is often used in the houses of parliament and congress. Essentially it involves meeting the meeting participants before the meeting formally or informally to discuss with them the objectives and main decision points, and to get their support for decisions or to understand their main objections. But before we even consider trying to get pre agreement, we should make sure that everyone is on the same page and that they are all going to come to the meeting in a spirit of decision making. Hence we syndicate to align objectives as well as understand positions and decision points. Of course, before we spend time on this process we need to ensure that we are going to have the right people in the room.

Participation frame

We need to understand clearly who needs to participate and how they are expected to participate. Deciding who to invite to a meeting can be difficult and can get you involved in office politics. Clearly we want to avoid this as much as possible and if we think that this is going to be the case we should ask senior managers to specify attendees. This is as simple as a quick meeting with the most senior person appropriate to explain what the meeting is for and to ask who should attend the meeting.

It is important to make sure that the decision makers, or those that you need to influence (such as gatekeepers and budget holders) are there so as to avoid having to go back to a higher authority or, worse, a second meeting with different people. To ensure this, just ask the decision makers to attend. If they are too busy you can point out that they are required at the meeting in order to make a decision, and so either the meeting is postponed (hence the decision is also postponed) or they attend. If they really can't attend then they should delegate someone who *has their authority* and you should check in writing that the person to whom they delegate has the authority to make a decision without referring to their manager, and most importantly that that manager will stand by the decision. If you can't get the decision makers to the meeting then, *don't have it.*

You must make sure that you set the meeting is at the right level, this allows for managers to delegate if necessary or decide to attend. But it must be at the level that will enable something to get done. It is important to level the participants, for example if the meeting has three directors and a managing director around the table, it is likely that the MD's views will carry purely on the basis of authority. Since you want the best outcome you should seek to avoid this degree of inequality, although this is more about knowing the participants than their grade in the organisation. If you can't ensure that everyone at the meeting is the right level, *don't have it.*

It usually helps to get the most senior people to attend a meeting if you can manage to get acceptance from at least one person at their level. But seniority is not always a mark of capability to make a good decision, or indeed understand the technicalities behind it. So you must ensure that the people coming to the meeting understand the purpose of the meeting, can understand the concepts and technicalities of the decision points and have authority to make recommendations or preferably decisions. Its a difficult balance which depends on the organisation and the personalities, which you will have to judge on a case by case basis.

Deciding who should be there is one difficulty but getting them there, and getting them there with a willingness to participate is another one. Try to avoid hangers on in the meeting, everyone in the meeting must be clear on the objectives and agenda and be there for a purpose. Furthermore you must ensure that everyone who needs to be there is there as you don't want to make a decision which is challenged later. Part of the purpose of the meeting is to ensure that the right people are involved in the process of decision making or providing information, its about getting buy in as well as getting a decision, so not having key people in the meeting is a risk. If you can't ensure that everyone at the meeting is the right level, *don't have it.*

Once you have the identified key participants then approach them before the meeting and syndicate the main decision points. This usually involves lots of coffee, and sometimes muffins. You won't always get agreement, but at least you will know what they are thinking and be able to structure your meeting accordingly (perhaps even changing the level of participation or pre-warning other attendees of potential stopping points). This ensures you have no surprises and can help to inoculate them against objections.

Finally, you should identify roles for the meeting participants, and in particular for yourself and any supporting colleagues you take along. Key roles and responsibilities are:

Chair - The chair's role is to manage the meeting agenda, and to move it along at a suitable pace. It is best, but not always possible, for the chair to not be a decision maker, as the chair should be in a position to arbitrate or assist in the resolution of sticky agenda points. In many committees the chair has a casting vote.

Minute taker - An extremely important role, and the one role that it is difficult to share with any other. A true and accurate record of the meeting and any decisions is essential and the minute taker should concentrate solely on this task.

Presenter - This is the person who is making the pitch, asking for a decision or disseminating information. Some times this role is shared with chairing the meeting, but it is useful to distinguish if possible.

Participant - All of the other people at the meeting. I have taken care here to label them as participants rather than attendees, because their participation, and engagement is required. The only time to include someone as an attendee who you know will not participate is where you want to make sure that they have had the opportunity to listen to the arguments, and information and to give the opportunity to participate, which will prevent potential problems later.

Once you have decided on who should attend, and what role they will play you can move forwards with thinking about the structure and timeframe of the meeting.

Time frame

You should state clearly the meeting duration, start time and, of course, location.

There are three simple questions here, that can have a major impact on the success of the meeting. How soon should the meeting take place, what time should it be scheduled for and how long is the meeting going to be? The answer to the first depends on a combination of factors, such as any deadlines, availability of participants and most importantly available time to prepare. Meetings at which significant decisions need to be made require planning and preparation, time is also required for syndication and so it is important to make sure that you have enough time to get everything in place to manage the meeting properly.

The availability of participants has an impact on meeting time, but if you book the meeting far enough in advance then this should not be a problem. Here follow some generalisations which may help you in planning the time of your next meeting. People are fresh in the morning, and usually motivated and receptive. This is the best time for decision making and brainstorming, but getting agreement may be more challenging. Generally this is true also for meetings earlier in the week. Meetings straight after lunch tend to provide opportunities to sleep-off lunch, and so don't expect a lot of participation, although this may be a good time to push through a decision against little resistance. Evening meetings tend to be quick as people want to get home, but they often overrun as people become tired and irascible.

They are not a good time for a meeting at all. Afternoon meetings will be slow, but can be productive, they are good times to disseminate information. In my opinion the best time for a meeting is just before morning coffee or just before lunch, there seems to be an urgency in getting to a resolution that is always useful. Try not to let the meetings overrun though or you will loose the participants to their cheese sandwich!!

Short meetings are more productive in so many ways. We can spend many hours in meetings, and we can waste a lot of time. Short and sweet meetings with targeted agendas and clear objectives are better. However, because of the way outlook works we have a habit of setting meetings to last for an hour. In general half hour, or even twenty minute meetings are better. But you need to set expectations that the meeting will be short, with the aim of coming to a decision or disseminating information, and no more. This takes discipline, but once you are in the habit of running meetings like this, and your meeting attendees are in the habit of participating in meetings like this then you will find a massive uptick in productivity.

Structure frame

The meeting should be structured to achieve the meeting objectives, We should ask ourselves what things we need to do, and in what order do we need to do them so that we get to where we want to at the end of the meeting. This allows us to produce an agenda. The agenda should state the the objectives clearly, and the order of discussion. It would be my recommendation never to include an AOB (Any Other Business) line in the agenda. The meeting should be focussed on the objectives stated, and if there is anything else to discuss that then that should be left for another meeting. AOB is an invitation for general discussion which is often off topic and wastes time or for discussion on a point which someone else is bringing to your meeting. Any relevant additional points should be on the agenda, and you can invite other agenda items when you set up the meeting to avoid the curse of AOB[1].

> **Sample meeting announcement**
> **Participants**: Adam, Jeremy, Sarah, Toni, Carlos
> **Date:** 21 Jan 2006, Start: 12:30; End: 13:30
> **Objective**: To reach an agreement on the budget for 2010
>
> **Agenda**
>
> - Review of minutes from last meeting
> - Status update
> - Review budget proposal and decision
> - Date of next meeting

In planning and structuring the meeting you should take time to prepare logistics. By this I mean who should attend, what time the meeting is to be and where it is. The decision of where the meeting is to be held depends often on room availability, but something to think about is the

---

[1]As a concession you may allow AOB at the start of the meeting. You can then re-cut the agenda to include items raised.

idea of 'playing at home'. In any sport there is a home advantage, and the same goes for meetings. Meeting in your office, or in a meeting room on your floor gives you the balance of power, and puts you in a strong position to drive the meeting. The other participants have to come to you, the meeting is therefore important enough to them to make the effort and spend the time and they will therefore more likely be active participants.

I once attended a meeting in a Japanese bank. Business meetings in Japan are very different to those anywhere else that I have been. This was a meeting to explain the services of the consultancy company that I was working at. The meeting had been organised by our Japanese partner, and they had defined the agenda. There were three of us, and about ten delegates form the bank, from the CIO and his direct reports. We sat on one side of a long table and they all squeezed along the other. Much of the meeting was conducted in Japanese, and it was most certainly conducted in 'Japanese style' (which I was to learn is a very specific way of doing things). Our partner introduced us by reading straight off of slides, of which the other meeting attendees had copies, and seemed to follow along (since they were written in Japanese, I could only look at the pictures). It was then my turn, and as I began talking I noticed that the CIO seemed interested in what I had to say, those to the immediate left and right of him seemed interested in what *he* had to say, and those at the very end of the table seemed a little disconnected and frankly quite sleepy.

I had no real way of engaging them, but I looked at them the end occasionally as I talked. One in particular was looking down at his slide deck, and not turning the page. His head was drooping somewhat. I looked away, at the other end of the line to concentrate for a second on getting some participation from that end, and suddenly my attention was drawn back to the other end of the table by a loud thud. The senior engineer at that end of the table had drifted off and fallen off of his chair. He got up, sat back on his chair and waited for me to continue. No-one said anything.

In order to help structure the meeting you should prepare meeting pack along with any other meeting materials. One way to drive a meeting is to prepare a slide deck that is printed out and given to each participant at the start of the meeting. This slide deck should include the following items:

- Agenda

- Objective

- One page with all the information needed for each decision

This last item is very important, as not all meeting participants will have come to the meeting prepared, and they will not all have all of the information that they need in order to make the decisions that they need to. Having one page that summarizes the required information in a straightforward format that is easy to understand ensures that everyone is making a decision from at least a common level of understanding, and information (and its information that *you* give them, which can be useful!!) .

> **Meeting Planning**
> Thinking of the next meeting that you are going to be running
> (if you are not running it, act as if you are) frame the meeting
> and prepare an announcement, an agenda and a meeting pack

6.2   The meeting

If you have prepared well, then running the meeting should
be relatively straightforward. You are clear about the objectives, agenda and running order, and you should have all of
the right people in the room. There are some last minute
preparations to carry out on the day of the meeting and it
is always a good idea to arrive early in order to:

- Arrange seating - who sits where, and next to whom?

- De-clutter room - so that there is nothing to distract
  delegates.

- Meet all participants as they arrive - and ensure that
  you know who they are, their name, and their role.

- Hand out the meeting pack - making sure that there
  is one for everyone.

- Check that any technology or demonstrations work as
  expected.

You should also think about the way you present yourself.
It may not seem as if it should be important but it is clear
that your appearance, confidence and manner make a difference to your ability to run the meeting effectively, and in
particular to control difficult situations and manage unruly
meeting attendees.

6.2.1 Conducting the meeting

There is one main rule for running a successful meeting - *stick to the agenda*. If you go off on a tangent then the meeting will not achieve your set objectives, and a lot of time will be wasted. Agendas can help when delegates try to take a meeting off topic or appear disinterested. Any attempt to derail the meeting can be challenged by bringing focus back to the stated agenda.

It is also extremely important to *stick to the timeframe*, and to ensure that the meeting starts and ends on time (it can also end early, but not start early, or late). Starting on time sets a professional and business like tone, and ensures that everyone is focussed. If the key participants are late you can wait a few minutes and then either start, or postpone the meeting. It is important to have everyone engaged in the meeting, as active participants and there are some ways you can achieve this, as we will see below, but they require everyone to be present. It is bad, but common practice to arrive late to meetings, but sometimes unavoidable. Ultimately it is your call. After a few times of starting a meetings on time, and assuming quorum[2] people generally work out that if they want to be involved then they need

---

[2]Meetings that are quorate have the right to make decisions on behalf of the meeting delegates even if not all of them can attend. You do need to agree what the basis for quorum is before the meeting and usually this will be either a certain percentage of people are present to make the decision or specific people are present. For recurring meetings such as steering meeting for example, I will establish the criteria for quorum at the first meeting. For others, I will just make a judgement call

to turn up on time. Only having 30 minutes to digest the information and make a decision focusses attention, and so ensuring that the timeframe is adequate and managed is very important. Try to make the meeting snappy and 'over before you know it' so that no-one is being distracted and looking at their watch waiting for the torture to end.

Did I mention the most important part of running a meeting? *Stick to the agenda*

Finally it is time for the meeting to take place. Even if you have prepared well the meeting won't run itself and they way in which you conduct and lead the meeting will define the success. Essentially a meeting is an opportunity to use your influencing and negotiation skills in a group setting. The meeting moves forwards in a linear sequence, with a beginning a middle and an end and then leads to a set of post meeting activities.

Introduction and gaining rapport

In the beginning you set the scene and set the meeting up to be successful. But before you start you have to begin, and in beginning you need to create a frame for decision making and collaboration. Your meeting has the objective of influencing the people around the table in a specific direction or towards a specific outcome. All of your communication and influencing skills will come in to play here, and you will need to extend them to work in a group setting not just for individuals. There are some tips in this chapter, and also in the chapter on powerful presentations that help with this.

The first thing to do in a group setting is to *create*

a general feeling of rapport throughout the group. This should be centered at you as the one who will be leading the group but should also include the feeling of collaboration and rapport between and amongst participants, as this helps to build an agreement oriented frame. Here is where you use the skills of communication and influence that we developed in the core part of this book to gain and and and maintain rapport with all participants.

Much of what we now know about building rapport has been focussed on the individual, and on understanding and knowing the way in which the individual behaves and responds. In a group setting it is not possible to focus on everyone all of the time, so we must use simple universal experiences to start the process. For example I will often start the meeting by discussing my journey, or the weather - which is one thing we can usually all agree on!! Here is an example of a simple yes set based introduction to a meeting.

> 'I don't know about you, but I always feel that meetings first thing in the morning seem to start the day off well. I know many of you had a difficult journey here today, and I thank you for making the effort to get here quite this early. I haven't been to this office before, but I found the walk from the station very therapeutic, particularly with it being such a clear and sunny day. This is actually quite a nice office, but despite the pleasant surroundings and the rather good coffee, but don't get too comfortable as I don't plan to keep you here for a

moment longer than is necessary, I'm sure that you all have other things to do. This is important however and we do need to get through all of the information and make a decision in the next 90 mins.'

'We are all here for a reason, and I know that we want to find a resolution today if we can. I'm sure you're thinking already about some of the key points but before we get to that I'd like to make sure that we are all clear of the objective....'

Without too much detailed analysis it is easy to see this as a set of universal experiences that all participants should be able to agree with, with a clear instruction at the end - 'We need to make a decision in 90 mins' (this is a SMART outcome!!). We can all agree, that its a nice office, that the weather is sunny, that the coffee is good, its early, it was a nice walk from the station, we all have other things to do, this is important, and that (ambiguously) we are all here for a reason. Notice also the usage of Visual, Kinesthetic and Auditory words to appeal to all submodality types (and the coffee has olfactory and gustatory elements too for those who are that way inclined). At this point everyone should be locked in to a single objective and in a frame to come to an agreement.

The juggling act that you have to perform, as the one who is driving the meeting, is to *maintain rapport with all participants throughout the meeting*. This requires you to be acutely aware of the responses of each participant to the things that you are saying and the things that they are saying to each other. You need to continually bring them back to you, the centre of attention and the hub of rapport.

Focussing all the time on the maintenance of rapport, you should *start the meeting by stating clearly the objectives*. These should be in the meeting pack, and I suggest writing it on a board or sticking it up on the wall so that it can become an anchor for the meeting. Any time someone moves off topic you can point at the objective, and say 'let's understand how this helps us achieve the objective'.

The next thing to do is to *ensure that everyone round the table knows who everyone else is, what their role in the meeting is* and how that matches with the meeting objectives. In particular the Chair, and the Minute-taker should be identified. It is usually a good idea to ask each participant to introduce themselves, and if you start you can set the tone, content and length of this (which should be short).

Next you should *explain the agenda*, the running order of the meeting, as this shows how you are going to achieve the meeting objective. If you have prepared well then no-one should challenge this and there should be no surprises. Do not give anyone an opportunity to change this, as your whole meeting plan depends on this agenda. We discuss how to deal with difficult people in a later section, for now just remember that you must *stick to the agenda*. You do this most easily if you have prepared a pack with pages in sequence of the agenda.

It is common for meeting attendees to flick through the meeting pack while you are talking to see what is on the other pages, and often to ask questions about these pages before you get there or after you have left them. I suggest that you stick to the agenda and say that you will answer that when you get to that point in the meeting. Resolutely, and politely, stick to the planned sequence of events. and follow the pack, *keep everyone on track*. After all, it's your meeting. Anything that crops up that is interesting but not relevant can be parked and discussed later. You need confidence and commitment of purpose to be able to say: 'That is an interesting point, lets discuss it off line'

It it very important to keep everyone engaged in the meeting, all of the time. Think of the meeting as a process of getting buy-in for a decision, and make sure that everyone is 'bought-in'. This can only happen when everyone is fully engaged. You may see participants drifting off (falling off of the chair asleep for example!!) or chatting between themselves. This means you have lost rapport, and in this case you need to directly address a question or a point to them using this an opportunity to build rapport once more. If someone is entirely disinterested in the meeting they should not be there and you can ask them 'are you the right person to be in this meeting?', in fact you can avoid this altogether by making sure that you do indeed have all of the right people in the meeting before you start.

Regardless of whether or not the meeting objectives have been achieved it is imperative to finish the meeting on time. This has a couple of effects, firstly if people know that you don't allow meetings to overrun then they will be happy to attend your meetings and participate, secondly giving a timescale to make a decision helps to ensure that a decision is made. So finish on time, and if you haven't achieved your outcomes, set out and agree the next steps very clearly. If you manage your meetings well, people will be happy to come to them and will come with a frame for agreement, or at least a frame for working on getting an agreement.

At the end of the meeting it is your job to pull everything together. You need to summarise the meeting, the actions, the decisions and any next steps. This should be stated, and then written down and circulated post meeting. Once this is done, then you can signal that the meeting is at an end by starting to pack up your papers, moving your chair back, saying 'thank-you' or breaking rapport in any number of other ways. Remember though it should be you or the Chair who ends the meeting, not one of the participants.

6.2.2 After the meeting

After the meeting all actions, decisions and next steps should be communicated. There is always a question about the extent and type of meeting minutes, and this really depends. The purpose of detailed minutes are to capture what was said by who in what context. Usually for business meetings this level of detail is not appropriate, and the time and effort taken to create suitably detailed minutes is usually best spent on other things. Gone are the days when every meeting had a secretary who took copious notes and wrote out detailed, line by line, scripts of the meeting. These kinds of minutes are usually not useful in the business context.

As consultants we have a duty to capture, report on and drive meeting outcomes. Decisions and actions should clearly be attributed to the appropriate person. You can add value by making sure that all actions are SMART, in particular time based and are tracked at each meeting and in the interim. I recommend keeping meeting minutes to a summary level, rather than the detail. Different environments do call for different approaches and you should look at best practice in your industry to ensure that you at least know what you are expected to do (even if you choose to do something different).

Sample meeting summary
Attendees: Adam, Toni, Carlos
Apologies: Sarah
Date: 21 Jan 2006, Start: 12:30; End: 13:30
Objective: To reach an agreement on the budget for 2010
Summary of key points

- Budget not agreed as it stands, The main issue was the extend of the IT spend. There was concern over the high cost of laptops (Toni) and the need for a faster Coms line (Carlos).

- All other budget items agreed

- It was also agreed that no further meeting would be necessary if the IT budget can be trimmed by 10%

Actions

- Toni to revert to committee by e-mail by 26th Jan with reduced specification and costs for Laptops

- Carlos to revert to commitee by e-mail by 30th Jan with detailed bandwidth requirements from Dev teams.

In this case there may have been heated discussion about the laptop quality, chosen supplier or requirements form the Dev team. This is not relevant, what is is the way in which the problems are going to be resolved. This is clear form the summary.

6.2.3 Dealing with difficult people

Meetings don't always go smoothly, and the main reason for this is that they have people in them! Sometimes, for various reasons people will be difficult, disinterested, disenchanted or disruptive. Since the main thrust of this guide to running meetings is to ensure that you are on track, then this section shows you how to remain on track in the face of adversity. This section is relevant to all of this book and is a skill that consultants need to develop, it just happens to appear in the meetings chapter because it has direct relevance to our discussions.

It helps to remember the three R's of dealing with difficult people. Rapport, Relevancy, Refer to a higher authority.

Rapport - It goes without saying, we like people who are like us. We are less likely to be difficult around people we like, although as many of us will no doubt attest children and loved ones seem to be the exceptions to this rule!! Having good rapport however can help us get over, through or around difficulties much better, and it is unlikely that someone with whom we have good rapport will want to be difficult just for the sake of it. There is likely a good reason, and in that case we may need to negotiate a shared objective to overcome the problem.

Relevancy - This is one of my favorite approaches. More often than not you can issue a relevancy challenge to sidestep a difficult issue. In the context of a meeting where the agenda and objectives are clear you are well within your rights to ask 'I'm not sure how that is relevant to achieving the objectives of this meeting'. Usually if the protagonist is just being difficult, it won't be. You can then just add 'let's get back on track'.

Refer to higher authority (or someone else) - in the event that nothing seems to work, you can offer to hand the problem over to someone who can deal with it. Your boss or your bosses boss, or a colleague. This helps to deflect the difficulty and sidestep it - if that is what you want to, or need to do.

In my teenage years I studied Karate. I was quite good, I had a brown belt and I fought for a local team. At a certain age there is nothing like putting on a crisp white suit and a dark coloured belt and prancing around the sportshall with an air of confidence. If bees had knees, I felt like them. My friend was a jiu jutsu green belt - a sort of less sporty for of judo, or so I thought. I often teased him as his black suit was always grubby, never ironed and it seemed to take him ages to progress. We had been training for the same time, and he was still three belts lower than me.

One day on our way home form the cinema together, we were approached by a mini-gang of overconfident thugs who as far as I could tell wanted to beat us up. Suffice it to say after a few choice words a fight ensued. I stood, in proud stance, waiting for the first assailant to make his move and as he came I struck out hard with a straight punch to his solar plexus. He went down, but so did I! I hit high and punched at his rib cage, my wrist bent, my knuckles hurt and I had met force with force and we both came off badly.

As I clutched my almost broken wrist I caught out of the corner of my eye my friend sidestepping one assailant and catapulting him five feet in the air, stepping round behind the second and tripping him to the ground, and then some-how moving to the right and then spinning to the left with the third assailant throwing him by his wrist and spinning him 360 degrees in mid air. My friend picked me up, and we walked off. He hadn't even broken a sweat, and his shirt was still 1980's style pristine. He looked at me and smiled and said 'Jiu jutsu Adam, the gentle art - use thier own force against them, it takes much less effort'. I joined his dojo the next week.

Included with the three R's are the EOON skills. These help you to enact Rapport, Relevancy and Referral, or can stand on their own as appropriate techniques for dealing with someone who is being difficult. Notice I don't say *head on* as this isn't the way forwards, I learnt a hard lesson about this, in head on encounters the strongest wins and you both get hurt. You want to try to apply principles of jiu jutsu and deflect any difficulties, using the opponents energy against them. Here are some ways to do this:

Emotion - You can ask, 'how do you think that makes me feel?' or 'Do you think in your heart of hearts that that is useful?'. Talk about how their position makes you, or the rest of the group feel 'Your stance makes me feel uncomfortable'. Or perhaps discuss how not getting to a resolution feels, 'I know that you want to get to a resolution'

Off-line - If all else fails, issue the relevancy challenge and take the discussion offline, to another meeting or a private meeting. 'I see your point, but I'm not sure that this is relevant here, lets take this offline'

Other delegates - This is a useful gambit, in that it uses a peer pressure approach. 'lets ask the group what they think'.

Negotiation Skills - And finally, there is a whole chapter in this book about how to get to a resolution through negotiation. Remember the key point is working towards a set of shared outcomes and goals that are mutually beneficial.

6.2.4 And Finally...

Successful people run successful meetings. In fact meetings are an excellent opportunity to impress your boss, or would be bosses or the client as they showcase your planning, decision making, organisation,summary, negotiation and delivery skills. In many cases a meeting that you organise will be the first and perhaps only place that a senior client or manager will see you in action, and impressions form these kind of encounters always count.

Successful meetings give rise to successful projects, and deliveries. Meetings can help identify requirements, set structures in place, make decisions that effect the project and create a momentum. If you want to deliver a project on time and in budget, you need to make sure that you hold the right meetings, with the right people, at the right time.

A meeting with a purpose is a successful meeting. No purpose = No meeting. Remember this, it is the most fundamental principle of consultancy.

Chapter 7

Asking the right questions

Consultants consult, right? There is a brilliant Dilbert cartoon that has Dogbert sitting on a hill talking about his work. He says 'I like to con people (pause), I like to insult people (pause), if you put con and insult together you get ... consult'. It's not really like that, is it? I have seen consultants, who think that they know best, ignoring client requests and suggestions. They take no notice of the client requirements, in fact don't even understand what the requirements are, and then treat them as stupid when they don't seem to like the recommendations or output of the consulting engagement. This is not consultancy, this is bullying, and the client never asks the consultant, or the consulting company back.

True consultants avoid this career and business limiting approach through adopting a more client oriented approach. But many still get stuck, because they don't actually understand what the client wants. This is usually because the client doesn't understand what they want either!! The key to success is to ask the right questions in the right way to get underneath the clients generalisations to the real nub of the problem, to the real requirement. This may seem difficult, in fact many consultants find this the hardest part of their job - delivery is relatively easy once you know what you have to deliver - but in fact if you use the exquisite communication skills that we have introduced in the first section of the book and focus on a few simple questioning techniques that I will show you here, you should find that this is easier than it appears.

7.1 The problem of non-specific language

When we communicate we often leave out lots of information and expect others to fill in the gaps. This is one of the things that we leave out ourselves when we think about communicating. Its not such a clever idea but it was Derrida [1980] who pointed out that the author of a text and the reader of a text have different meanings of the same text. What I say, and what you understand are not the same. This is very important in all interactions, and it is particularly important in the artful art of asking questions.

There are three ways in which we tend to simplify our experiences when we talk about them.

- Distortion - we create meaning by ignoring some pieces

of information while concentrating on others.

- Generalisation - we make broad claims based upon little evidence.

- Deletion - we leave bits of information out.

These simplifications were first codified in the analysis of the language of therapy patients [Bandler and Grinder, 1979] but are generally applicable to any form of communication in any context, especially business[1].   I am sure that you have a number of examples where things have been left out of the conversation, or left unsaid, or assumed that should have been mentioned, or should not have been assumed, and have caused issues.   This is where asking the right questions can help to get underneath issues to real problems, issues and requirements.

The Simplified meta-model

I once was discussing a business process with a set of users. The key was to automate as much as possible using a new system. I knew that I couldn't automate everything on day-one go-live, and I wanted to understand what the most important pieces were. We were talking about order processing, and they said quite clearly that they never processed any part of the orders manually. I collected all of the other details about the current automated process and with help delivered the system on go-live day. That happened to be the

---

[1]There is a certain sense in which a consultant could be thought of as a counsellor or therapist anyway!!

day that the occasional client form South Africa made in an order. This client, due to general communication problems across the african subcontinent, always faxed a confirmation of the order, which had to be scanned, and then entered into the system - manually!! We didn't have a way of entering the order at all, and weren't able to take the business. This sort of thing happens a great deal in consultancy.

Of course, in my defence I could argue that it is impossible to know what it was that I didn't know, and that the users all confirmed that there were no manual processes. But the problem stems from not recognising the potential distortions, deletions and generalisations and not asking the right questions to uncover what it is that we don't know. It is my responsibility to identify the pointers to simplifications and to use the correct questioning to uncover the hidden meanings and lost information.

In order to make sure that I really did have all of the information all I had to do was ask, 'What, never? You can't think of any examples where you have processed this manually?'

Here is another example of a simplification.

> **Client:** *'I can't do my job, the system doesn't work'*
> **Consultant:** *'What, never?'*
> **Client:** *'Well, not really, sometimes.'*
> **Consultant:** *'In which ways does the system not working prevent you doing your job'*
> **Client:** *Well, actually I really hate the interface, and I can't find out how to everything I need*

> *to. It frustrates me and I get fed up so I do it*
> *manually*

In this example, the client is distorting the facts and generalising. They are clearly doing their job, just maybe not as effectively as they could be because of issues with the system. There is a cause-effect relationship here that needs to be understood, and in most cases the stated cause is not the cause of the problem. By asking a question which leads the client to specify the problem the real issues with the system emerge, and appear to be a user interface problem, or potentially a training problem.

> **Consultant:** *'Would it be a help if I worked with*
> *you to see what you couldn't do, and worked out*
> *what you could do, and how to do it'*

Users often tell you how they feel about systems, projects, deliverables, colleagues and sometimes things a little more personal. We must remember that consultancy requires both technical and an interpersonal skills. In particular, getting the most out of someone often requires us to understand the emotional and motivational depths of a problem or issue before we can begin to address any direct, functional issues. As I said, a consultant is often times a counsellor, and having a good deal of emotional intelligence [Goleman, 1996] is not enough without the tools to get underneath and understand the details of the issues. For example if a client says:

> *'I feel fed up.'*
> You might ask, *'About what exactly?'*

Notice here the question isn't 'why?', because the answer to this question usually comes with a whole load of unnecessary fluff, and usually winging : ' Because its boring and no-one listens to me'. What is more useful is the specific questioning above, and the resulting specific answer: 'well, I'm fed up with the repetitiveness of the task'.

Using this method of questioning, you can not only find out the specifics of issues, requirements or problems but you can act as a true consultant and become an *agent of change*.

> 'I just can't get it done in a day.'
> *'what stops you?'*
> 'There is always too much to do'
> *'Always?'*
> 'Well, sometimes'
> *'What is special about those times when there is too much to do?'*

Are you beginning to see just how effective this questioning approach can be? It is designed not only to get specific requirements but also to challenge the client's model of the way things appear to be, and to break down any limitations in thinking that hamper new ways of doing things and creative thinking.

> 'Well, at the end of the month the transaction volumes really increase'
> *'Ok, since you know that this will happen regularly is there something that you can pre-arrange to help you cope with the volume'*

'Well, we could use an extra pair of hands on
that day, but that's not possible'
'What prevents you finding an extra pair of hands?'
'My boss would never allocate someone'
'Have you asked?'
'No'
'What would happen if you did?

This way of questioning makes way for outcome driven
thinking - chunking up to try to establish the desired outcome and find other solutions that address the outcome,
not the problem. An alternative scenario for the transaction processing problem would be to focus on the desired
result, to have all transactions processed by the end of the
month. As you can see, there are other ways of addressing
the problem.

'Well, at the end of the month the transaction
volumes really increase'
*'Ok, and do you need to process all of those
transactions on the same day'*
'Yes, they all come in at the end of the month'
'all of them? On the same day? '
'Well, no, quite a few come in during the last
week, in dribs and drabs'
'Do you process them when they come in?'
'No'
'Can you? what would happen if you did?

This approach to questioning is based on the meta-
model, which can be found in full in *The structure of magic*

Too (much, many, expensive..);	Compared to what?
Nouns (things, people, places..); 'They don't understand me'	Who specifically (doesn't understand you)?
Verbs (doing words); 'I feel bored'	How, specifically (do you feel bored)?
Negatives (shouldn't, mustn't, can't)	What would happen if you did? What prevents it?
Generalisations (always, never)	Always? Never?

[Bandler and Grinder, 1979]. In complete form the meta-model further subcategorises each of distortion, deletion and generalisation further. However It is sufficient for our needs here for the purposes of a client interview, to understand five rules of thumb known as the simplified meta-model, or the precision model [Laborde, 2001].

Here are some examples:

> *It is too much effort to do it this way* - Compared to what?
>
> *They keep putting obstacles in my way.* - Who specifically puts obstacles in your way?
>
> *I feel like it can't be done.* - How specifically do you feel it can't be done?
>
> *I can't seem to get it done.* - What would happen if you did? What prevents you?
>
> *I never get to be involved in these things.* - What, never?

Of course one question may lead to another distortion,

generalisation or deletion, and you will need to continue to dig underneath the statements to get to the real issues and problems. The key to this level of questioning is to be more and more specific, and follow a line of questioning to its logical conclusion. Here is an example of how the meta-model can lead to the establishment of an appropriate outcome:

> *I feel useless.*
> How specifically?
> *Well, I feel useless because they don't give me any responsible work.*
> Who specifically are 'they'?
> *It's my boss, he never gives me any responsible work.*
> Never?
> *Well, he did last year.*
> And what happened when he did?
> *I got the work done, but had to do a presentation at the end, and I fluffed that really badly. Since then I haven't felt able to take any similar work on just in case I have to give a presentation.*
> Well, if we were to find a way to work together on your presentation confidence and skills, then you would be able to take on that work, wouldn't you?
> *Yes.* And how would that make you feel?
> *Great.*

> **Exercise**
> Give the meta-model questions that you would use to uncover the deeper structure in these statements:
>
> *I can't do it.*
> *I am not confident.*
> *That button has to be blue*
> *We must change the process to accommodate Monday's new requirements*
> *No-one listens to my point of view.*
> *It's too hard get it right all of the time.*

7.2 Requirements gathering

The requirements gathering process usually starts with an interview with the potential users, or the the eventual recipients of the outcomes of your consultancy exercise, the stakeholders. Knowing what you now know about communication you will understand that just asking simple questions is not actually going to get to the true requirements. A usual approach to gathering requirements is to capture what is said and then to present that back to the stakeholders for agreement. This is the cause of many project failures.

Stakeholders have a habit of giving you their solution to a problem in the guise of a requirement. Inexperienced consultants have a habit of writing this down, and then when they find that there are better ways of achieving the outcome required by the stakeholder they are unable to implement it because they have already agreed the solution essentially as part of the requirement.

I was once working on the delivery of a front end, user

interface, to some clients which was to connect to a complex database system and was to be used for high volume data entry and cleaning tasks. I arrived at the first meeting to discuss what was required to find a projector and screen in the room. Rather than discussing the requirements, I was shown an interface that the users had built themselves, using a RAD [2] tool. By itself this was excellent, as all I had to do was create something that was exactly like this front end and then I would have matched their solution. However I could see straight away that the way that they had chosen to implement this would not address many of the issues that I knew were coming up. I was now in a difficult position, if I delivered exactly their interface it would show that I had listened, but it would not work. Of course convincing them of this was going to be difficult.

Where possible we need to conduct the requirements gathering process from an outcome oriented frame. The key to this is to try and find out, specifically, what the stakeholder is trying to achieve, **not** what they want. Once you find out what they want to achieve, then you can work with them to agree a way of achieving it.

There is also an element of negotiation in each requirements gathering session. The client will state the requirement, and then together you will have to re-state it in a way that makes sense for the delivery of the project. For example, in looking to outsource some compute requirements to

---

[2]Rapid Application Development - an approach to quickly building IT systems which focusses on producing prototypes which get closer and closer to the final system, very popular in the 1990's.

a datacentre away from head office I was once told that a round trip time for communication between the datacentre and head office should be less than 10 milliseconds. I wrote this down and stated it back, making clear that I had the requirement correct. Of course, this is practically impossible, and so I tried to get to the required outcome by asking some questions.

It transpired that there were some critical calculations that were already near their deadline and that the worry was that sending them off to an outside datacentre would just be another factor in any further delays. I pointed out that calculations themselves took over 5 minutes each, and so we agreed that we could conceivably add half a second of overhead and it would not be noticed. This opened up datacentres that were hundreds of miles away and much more cost effective in terms of the solution. The client was bought-in to the requirement and understood the justification. When the requirements document came back for sign-off, there were no problems with this particular requirement.

You are the consultant, and should be adding value to the requirements gathering exercise by bringing your experience and expertise to the table to ensure that the requirements are correct, and well formed[3] or SMART. This essentially means that they should be achievable (by the individual, the organisation, the consultant), that it should be clear what the criteria for success is, and that the conse-

---

[3]We have discussed Well formedness criteria in the negotiation chapter and you can find a summary in the supplementary material.

quences of achieving them are understood. This is key to establishing good criteria that support project success.

Exercise
Take a requirement that you have recently gathered (it could be for a client, or for yourself -' I need a new TV', for example) - and put it through the well- formedness conditions.

Requirements are usually gathered in a formal interview. Requirements gathering is a process, which requires at least two participants and requires elements of negotiation and creativity to get to an agreed set of requirements with success criteria that can form the basis of a project specification. This is an interpersonal process, and as such all of the exquisite communication skills that you built in the first section apply. Specifically, you need buy-in and for buy-in you need a strong, positive relationship. This means that you need rapport. Gaining and maintaining good rapport with the clients is absolutely necessary for a successful outcome in the requirements gathering process.

Throughout the interview process, and in fact throughout your interaction with the client, your relationship with them will benefit from the process of active listening. This is a simple set of techniques that helps you build rapport with the client, by giving them the comfort that you really are listening to them. People really like to feel that they are being heard.

7.3 Active listening

Active listening is a way of listening and responding to another person that improves mutual understanding. Often when people talk to each other, they don't listen attentively. They are often distracted, half listening, half thinking about something else. While someone is talking, the listener is often busy formulating a response to what is being said. They assume that they have heard what is being said repeatedly before, so rather than paying attention, they focus on how they can respond.

Particularly valuable in conflict or stressful situations, active listening is a structured form of listening and responding that focuses the attention on the person speaking. The basic technique is that the listener pays full attention to the speaker, and then repeats, in the listener's own words, what she thinks the speaker has said. An important point here is that the listener does not have to actually agree that what the speaker has said is correct or valid, and the listener certainly should not judge what has been said; they must just state what they think the speaker said. This helps to build rapport by giving the speaker assurance that the listener really understood. And it gives the opportunity for further explanation if the listener did not understand.

It helps too if the listener re-interprets the speaker's words in terms of feelings. And so, instead of just repeating what was said, the active listener might also say, 'I gather that you felt annoyed when...' This means that the listener is able to indicate that he or she also understood the speaker's emotional response to the event.

An example of active listening would be:

> **Client:** *I just get bored with doing the same tasks over and over again, I feel that I'm not valued.*
>
> **Consultant**: *So what you are telling me is that the process is repetitive and you find it boring, and that because of this you feel that your worth to the organisation is not recognised?*

Active listening is a valuable tool that can help you build rapport and question the client more easily. Since aim of the client interview is to establish the requirements it is very important then that you are agreeing on what those requirements are. A key part of the client interview is to really try to get underneath the surface structure of what is being asked for and if at all possible, focus on the true required outcome. This can be done through a combination of active listening and use of the Meta-model questions .

A quiet word of warning

The questioning technique outlined here can be very disconcerting and must be handled with care. When I first learned the meta model I found that with brusk, direct questioning I could make people very uncomfortable. People are not used to being challenged in such a compelling way, and most never ask themselves these types of questions. It is part of your job as a consultant to be challenging, but you certainly don't want to come across as aggressive or dismissive. It is best not to fire off these questions one after another, and do try to use openers such as 'I wonder if... (you could tell me what would happen if you did?)' or 'Do you think you could tell me what.... (specifically, makes it difficult for you?)' which make the questioning seem less direct. Most importantly you should have good rapport with the interviewee, and you must use your sensory acuity to be aware of how your questioning is being received.

Projects often fail, even when they match the stated requirements, because they don't address the true requirements. When the final delivery arrives it doesn't do what was actually wanted, what it was that would make the clients job easier, or what would truly create efficiency. But you won't know what will do this until you have asked the right questions. Asking the right questions, in the right way is a powerful skill of the consultant, and those who can do this well are able to create sets of requirements that address the true needs of the client, and more importantly can create momentum for changing the way that things are done and thought about. I hope you enjoy using the techniques and tools here, they can be fun and rewarding and open up, for both you and the client, new worlds and ideas.

Chapter 8

Creating a winning proposal

8.1 What is a proposal for?

Proposals are part and parcel of the consultants toolbox, and they form a large part of the work that a consultant does. In this chapter we won't be distinguishing between a proposal that is written to win a contract of work with a client, and a proposal to carry out work that is delivered as part of a cleint engagement. Essentially they are the same thing, it is just that salespeople have more of a hand in the former than the latter!! Ultimately the proposal is the statement of what it is that you will do, how you will deliver it and how it will be measured, this is the same if you are initiating a new project inside an organisation or trying to sell consultancy to a new client.

I have seen many very poor proposals. Usually they are filled with buzzwords, too much technical detail which seems to be to demonstrate how clever the proposal writer is, and very rarely tell me what I will be getting (although they are happy to tell me what it will cost). Like it or not a true proposal is an element of the sales process, it should create a sense of confidence that the project can be delivered and should sell to the reader the approach and of course the proposer (you, or your company).

This brings us to the question of the true purpose of a proposal. Of course the ultimate aim of the proposal is to win the project, the business, the promotion or whatever it is that you are proposing. If you are offered the opportunity to create a proposal then you know that you are close to winning the work, of course there may be competitors but the question is how to make your proposal the one that they choose. The answer is **not** by having the best price - you have to have the best proposal.

In having a proposal accepted, you essentially gain agreement (at least conceptually) on the approach that you plan to take, and on the deliverables and measures of success. At a high level then acceptance of the proposal gives you a mandate to proceed in the way that you have stated. Which means that the proposal must contain a true and accurate view of how you are going to deliver, including timelines and possibly even high level milestones.

The proposal starts with a description of the problem that needs to be resolved and the purpose of the project, and then details ways of addressing the problems and achieving the objectives. This gives an opportunity for the client to ensure that you really do uinderstand the problem, and to give them confidence that everything that follows is meaningful in relation to achieveing the objectives. The proposal serves as a strong confidence builder and a strong statement of credability.

So summarise, the purpose of the proposal is to:

- Communicate your competence to the decision makers.

- Clarify understanding, yours and theirs.

- Define objectives (and deliverables[1] - if you must).

- Establish timelines.

- State the value of the work to the client.

- Gain conceptual agreement on the approach.

- Win the business.

It is instructive to put yourself in the shoes of the key decision maker, the person who will decide whether or not to accept the proposal. If you think about what they will be looking for then you will be able to craft your proposal to suit thier needs. They are going to put themselves in your hands to deliver this project and so they will, above all, be wondering if they can trust you, and your consultancy firm. They will be interested in your competencies, and your experience, they will want to know *who* is going to deliver the project and what guarantees they have that the

---

[1]To be avoided if at all possible - we discuss this a little later on

project will finish on time with all objectives covered. Of course they will want to know whet they are getting for thier money, and clearly how much in terms of money or effort, it is going to cost. Above all they will want to know if you understand them, their organisation and their particular needs. You should bear this in mind as you tell your story.

8.2 Every proposal tells a story

A proposal, like any good story, consists of a beginning, a middle and an end. It should be a compelling read that leads the decision mazker through the decision making process, with each step contributing to the overall plot and ultimately making sure that by the time the decision maker gets to the pricing section, it won't even matter!! Sometimes it really does work like this, usually though there are budgetary constraints, and often there are bits of the proposal that just don't sit quite right.

Nonetheless, the story is simple, it essentially goes like this for all proposals:

Once upon a time you had a problem that you needed solving. You asked a consultancy to come along and help you understand the problem and then propose a solution. We understand this problem (Background statement), *we know what you want* (Objectives). *We have experience of solving this problem* (Staffing, case studies) *so it will be straightforward for us, and when we solve this problem it will give you enormous benefit* (Value statement). *We propose to solve the problem in one of two ways* (Approach,

Options), *as long as certain things take place* (Assumptions and Accountabilities) *and you can choose the more complete option for one price and the quick start option for a lower price* (Option oriented pricing).

It becomes compelling if the sections are well written. Each section is an opportunity to negate the good work that has come before it it getting to the proposal writing stage as well as the written sections, and so must be carefully planned and thought out.

Introduction

The introduction is the opportunity to show that we have been listening to the client and that we understand the problem. If we can understand the problem this shows that we have either come accross it before or are clever enough to be able to solve it. Not understanding the clients problem (or worse, choosing not to) are immediate turn-off's for the client ' I wouldn't choose them, they don't even understand what we want!!'. So, in the introducton we introduce the problem and give a review of how we came to be at this point, with all factors and features of the problem discussed (at a high level, we would also give a very high level statement of the obejctives of the project, but leave detail to a later section- this is the background statement).

Here, or in a seperate section, you would also state the value for the project to the client. This serves two purposes, first it shows the client that you really do understand the project and what it means for them, the second is that it helps to establish a price if you already agree on the value.

Objectives

The next section is the statement of the objectives. The objectives define the purpose of the project, and if there is no purpose, well, there is no project. Pulling objectives out and setting them up in a seperate section is valuable as it means that you can then drive the rest of the proposal back to the objectives. These objectives should be SMART, or well formed and should have been agreed by the client before they appear in the proposal - there should be no surprises here. It is also important to keep them chunked up to a high level, so that they are easy to grasp and don't get bogged down in the detail.

This continues the story - 'we know what you want to achieve' and a small set of high level objectives that are repeatable and understandable often become a mantra for the project. You will know that this has been successful when you hear your client saying things like:

> 'We need to get this project done as it will help us double productivity, drive up sales by a further 50% and increase our market presence in europe by 25%'

All the best things come in threes...

Once the objectives have been listed, then they should be turned into outcomes. Outcomes are usually much SMARTer than objectives and are often more granular. You should ask yourself *what outcomes do I need in order to achieve these objectives?* to assist in identifying correct outcomes. Outcomes drive deliverables. Deliverables drive plans. Deliverables are tangable, usually documents or software or similar - something that you can touch and feel and see. They give evidence that the engagement has resulted in something, and are very good ways of tying up outcomes, plans and milestones. For example if the outcome is a new piece of software, the deliverables may be sets of interfaces, core components, and documentation. The plan would have a work package for each of these deliverables. This is great (essential) for a project, and for detailed plans but it could be debated (and it is my view) that deliverables should not be included in the proposal. It is very important to remember that the proposal is not the project plan, and that the planning exercise should take place following a requirements gathering exercise, as part of the proejct- which the proposal is designed to help you win.

Focussing on outcomes in the proposal gives an opportunity for you to reshape the project as it progresses, to deliver only that which is absolutely required and not waste time on unnecessary documents (but to make sure that you do provide necessary ones). Imagine, for example, that you have an outcome which is to increase sales by 25%, you could state a deliverable as a marketing plan but when you arrive on site you find that the real way to increase sales is to train the sales team to handle calls better. In this case you can achieve the outcome with a different deliverable, yet if it's in the proposal you will have to do the marketing plan anyway, even though its not relevant and wastes time.

My advice is to avoid deliverables in the proposal, and only stipulate them in the plan when you know unequivicably that they must be produced. Instead focus on a well thought out and agreed set of outcomes. This is not always possible, as sometimes the deliverables are obvious or stipluated as a requirement, but it is desirable.

Approach

In the Approach section you have the opportunity to say how you will achieve the outcomes. In it you describe the project order and process at a high level. Here is where you start thinking about routes to the desired outcomes, and options for various complexity and completeness of deliverables. For example if the outcome is to provide a remotely accessible front end (user interface), you could offer to configure a solution which required users to log in to a central server, or you could offer to build front ends that ran on users computers. The latter would require more work, and would achieve the outcomes but may have other benefits that are more valuable, such as branding and market positioning.

The approach should be set out clearly, step by step, so that the decision maker can understand it, and the different options should be outlined. It is important to remember that this is **is not a project plan** and so a general approach not a detailed work package breakdown is required. You can give timescales that are approximate and milestones relating to the completion of each step but don't be pushed in to anything more specific, as once its written down you will very likely be held to account if you don't achieve it.

Staffing

The staffing section is important in creating a credible story, it explains who will do it and the relevant experience that they have to do the work. There is a delicate balance here as you need to ensure that the customer has confidence in your ability to deliver, but equally you don't want to be constrained by committing staff that may not be available (especially if they take a long time to make their mind up). This section should talk about the benefits of the consultancy, and the credibility of the consultancy, stressing that the client is being offered the consultancy to deliver the project, not the person. Admittedly the delivery will likely be through the person, but not exclusively. This is also a good point to state roles and responsibilities for the staff who will be on site.

Assumptions and accountabilities

Remembering that this is a proposal and not a project initiation document, then this section is the place where you should state risks and issues and their mitigation. There are only two approaches to risk management allowed in the proposal: Risks are either within someone's control in which case you or the client have to accept them and become accountable for them, or they are not under anyone's control in which case you have to assume that that they will not occur. Most of the assumptions will relate to things that you need in order to to to ensure that the objectives can be delivered. The proposal should include these in the assumptions section.

In particular here you should state things that if you don't have will prevent you delivering the project, and are outside of your control. For example, access to the building, a desk and a computer on day 1 are usually useful things to assume (especially on a short term project) as in my experience these can take sometimes weeks to organise. More importantly would be access to the right people at the right time. This can also be very difficult to arrange as people are busy, but stating this as an assumption ensures that this is in the clients mind. Better would be to state a schedule or minimum amount of contact per week.

By accepting the proposal the client implicitly accepts the assumptions contained within it (I have never had a client negotiate the assumptions). So this then becomes an implicit contract around accountabilities, which essentially says that you will keep to your side of the bargain (deliver) if they will too. If you are unable to deliver then you are responsible, except in the eventuality that the assumptions that you made about the involvement from the client's organisation were not able to be met. This is not a 'get-out' clause, and you must make every effort to deliver the project whatever the circumstances, but as soon as you notice things slipping you should meet the client and discuss ways in which they can meet the assumptions stated in the proposal. This is good project risk management, and should be part of the service that you provide.

Options and pricing

When we put the approach section of the proposal together we made sure to put in place some options in terms of the way in which the objectives can be met. This is the section to state the cost of each one. The aim here is to have two or three different options to allow the client to have a choice. This is a classic double bind situation in which the client is asked to choose from two options, both of which result in the same underlying choice - you are selected deliver the proposal [2].

Presenting options in this way, with different prices, then allows the client to pick the option that is within budget rather than trying to fit something into a budget that is just too costly. If you have priced fairly, put your proposal together well, and made it clear what is included in each option, there should be no need to negotiate. If the client wants a lower price, they can have a lower priced option. Usually you will be expected to negotiate as a matter of pride for the other side, but if this is the case then you can remove some of the deliverables to help justify the lower value. If you do expect to have to reduce prices, then make sure your initial anchor is above the target, and always offer lower priced options before negotiation. This is the concept of value based pricing - that price should be based upon value to the customer not effort expended [Weiss, 2003].

In deciding on the initial price you should think about

---

[2]Of course the client is at liberty to choose not to accept any of your options, but if you have a compelling story this is less likely, assuming they have budget and buying power that is

the value that this project offers. If a project saves a trading desk £1.5M then it would be reasonable to ask for a proportion (say 25%) of that as your reward. This would be the value of the project. You can get stuck in this idea that you price a project on effort expended, but this is not how traders get rewarded. They make deals and take a margin on the deal. With luck and good judgement it can take only a few minutes to make £1.5M. If you price based upon effort then you can only make more money by doing more work. That doesn't seem sensible to me.

Ancillary information

This section provides supporting information only, such as Staff CV's and any background information that would be useful. The client will want to buy experience and knowledge. That is the experience and knowledge of the company not just of the individual, so in this section you would place well crafted and targeted case studies that demonstrate the capabilities, and experience of the company. Only pick those that clearly illustrate and back up your experience and do make sure that they are clear, concise, relevant and short.

8.3   The purpose of a proposal

The proposal is a key part in the sales cycle, and it gives the client confidence that you know what you are doing. Usually, being asked to make a proposal is a clear signal form the client that you are in the running for a project and if you are an internal consultant, a proposal is usually a clear signal that the decision maker is keen to progress to the next steps. If you have won the right to make a proposal, you need to do a good job, hopefully the advice in this chapter can help you with that.

It is important to remember that the proposal is not a sales document, it needs to stipulate the outcomes of the project and describe how you will achieve them. It defines the criteria for measuring success and it defines the options for delivery and payment, and it serves as an ongoing template for the project. If at all possible it should be delivered in person and you should take the client through the proposal rather than have them read it independantly. This way you will be able to clarify any misunderstandings that may arise and steer the reading of the proposal. Ultimately the proposal is there to create buy-in for your approach.

The proposal is not there to create a relationship, or to sell the recommended approach, this is the salesman's job. It is not a sales document, and although it does, by itself, create a sense of confidence and validity in your company and your capability. This is a happy accident and should not be the objective. By the time you get to the proposal stage, much of the sales process should have been completed. The next steps are usually to close the client on one of the options at a given price, and this is (again) the job of the salesman. It is your job to create a compelling, accurate, clear, concise proposal which you can confidently deliver to, because you will ultimately be held to account for the estimates and deliverables that you have stated in your options.

CHAPTER 8. CREATING A WINNING PROPOSAL

Chapter 9

Powerful Presentations

In a small village, not so far away from here, at a time not so long ago, there was a very wise man. This wise man was really wise and he knew the answers to all the questions the villagers could ask. No one had ever asked a question that the wise man couldnt answer. In this small village there was also a little boy and, as little boys usually do, he asked lots of questions. When he had a question that no one else could answer, he would go to the wise man and every time, the wise man gave the little boy an answer. Eventually it became a challenge for the boy to come up with a question that the wise man couldnt answer, but no matter how hard he tried, he couldnt find one.

One day, whilst walking in the woods, the boy came across a small bird, which gave him an idea. He would capture the little bird and to take it to the wise man. He would hide the little bird in his hands and ask the wise man if what he had in his hands was dead or alive. If the wise man would say alive, he would squeeze his hands and the bird would be dead. If the wise man would say dead, the boy would open his hands and let the bird fly away, alive. This way he would find a question that the wise man could not answer.

It has been said that a good presentation is like a good coffee [1] in that the flavour of the coffee depends on the barista, not the beans or the grinder, the milk and especially not the particular chain whose space and tables you use when you drink it. I like this metaphor, doubly, because I like to think of a good presentation as a double expresso - a short, snappy, meaningful pick-me-up that fills you with enthusiasm, and tastes good!! This chapter focusses on one of the most important skills of a consultant, getting your message across with a presentation. This could be a presentation to a group to or an individual, the principles are the same, although we will focus more here on group presentations and the additional skills and capabilities required to create a powerful presentation that people remember. Coffee anyone?

9.1 Planning

You will find that there is one key theme in this book - Planning. I was once on a communication skills course with a bunch of interesting people from a variety of walks of life and fields. As you do on these courses, we were asked to turn to the person to the left and right of you, introduce ourselves and say what we wanted out of the course. The

---

[1]/www.presentationhelper.co.uk/presentation-espresso.htm

chap to the right of me was a lawyer, the one on the left told me that he was a comedian. I asked him what he was doing on the course and he said 'because I'm not actually very funny' (which I thought was hilarious, and he said that that was probably the funniest thing he had said in six months).

Delving into the problem it seemed that he had pitched up at the local open mike night, had a few beers, been pushed on stage by his mates and had the audience in stitches. He had been booked there and then on the spot for a 20 min slot in the club later that month and had died on stage. I asked him why, and he honestly said that he had no idea what he was going to say when he got on stage and so sometimes he was funny and sometimes he wasn't. Most recently not!! I said that he was on the wrong course, and he needed to prepare his 20 mins, he needed to pre-pare jokes, structure, stage craft, actions etc. I don't think the course instructor was very impressed with me, as the non-comedian thanked me, left the course at lunchtime and asked for his money back!!

A presentation is a performance and just as you wouldn't expect to do a great comedy set without meticulous plan-ning, you will not be able to carry off a great presentation without a good deal of effort in the preparation. You need to prepare your key messages, the way you are going to engage the audience, where you are going to stand, what aids you are going to use and a whole host of other things. Don't expect, even with a lot of experience, to be great off the cuff. And even when you are, don't expect that to be re-peatable anytime soon. Essentially, if you prepare well then you take out the risk and randomness in the quality of your presentation and performance.

Preparation for a presentation has many of the same essential elements as preparing for a meeting, which we discussed in chapter 6. Just as I made clear in that chapter, the first thing to think about is the purpose of the presentation. You have to establish the true objectives, ask yourself 'what do I want to achieve in this presentation?' and if you are not satisfied with the answer then you should think carefully whether the presentation is valuable. *If there is no purpose there should be no presentation!!* Presentations are an opportunity to stand in front of an attentive, relevant and interested audience and get your message across to them. You really need to be clear of what that message is. Write the message down clearly in a single sentence, and keep going back to it to ensure that your presentation supports your message. It is always a good idea to check the message and that the presentation is 'on message' with colleagues.

Presentations broadly split in to three types:

Explanatory presentations seek to explain ideas and concepts to the audience. Lectures are the archetypal explanatory presentation, and you find the lecture format being used in conferences as well as in smaller meetings where the purpose is to clarify, explain and help the audience understand. In preparing these presentations you need to think like a teacher, and try to construct your story in logical chunks that are easily grasped, leading to the required conclusions.

Informative presentations seek to inform, there shouldn't

be too much to explain here, this is about giving information, knowledge and experiences to the audience who can take assimilate and process them without your help in structuring an argument or necessarily drawing conclusions (although this is a good idea as the conclusion will serve to reenforce your message).

Sales presentations combine elements of information and explanation with a strong message. The aim of the sales presentation is to convince the audience to make a purchase (physically or conceptually), to buy your product or idea. To do this you need to tell a compelling story, with an explanation of whatever you are selling and its key features, evidence of it's quality and a reasoned and targeted argument which compels the audience to buy. Most presentations fall into this category, as even when you think you are not selling anything, you are selling a message, a set of ideas, a concept and of course whether you like it or not you are selling yourself.

The type of presentation you are creating will steer your preparation of material, how you structure the presentation and your message. There is also an audience in the room that you need to engage, convince and take along with you. It helps if you remember this, try to understand where they are coming from, and what there interests will be. This is a true skill, to be able to engage an entire audience for a whole presentation, and it starts with knowing your audience. In particular you must be aware of the level of knowledge about the subject and pitch at this level. For example you may deliver a presentation on Cloud computing to a set of CIO's who will want to know what Cloud computing is, and how they can exploit it to save money. A set of technologists however may be interested in the technical details of how you have exploited virtualisation to create a cloud system. Ultimately it is up to you to make decisions about the level of detail required to get your message across.

Every presentation tells a story, you must decide what story you wish to tell. The story has a beginning, a middle and and like a perfect cadence[2] should have a resolution at the end that clearly indicates to the audience that the story is finished. Of course, during your story you can have cliff hangers and leave things open until later, that is what makes a story exciting. People are more likely to remember a presentation when it has been exciting. Think about this as you prepare the presentation, and think of your story.

For example you could tell a story of a successful project delivery, or an unsuccessful one. In a sales presentation you could create a story with a possible future (a fiction - surely not in sales). In a presentation that is informational, where you want to get across ideas and knowledge the story is one of development of those ideas from simple concepts to the fully worked up idea. Many deeply complex ideas are simple when explained through the history of their development, I remember when I learnt about the concepts of

---

[2]Classical music is very picky, and has stipulated lots of rules about how music should be. They call it harmony. One of the rules is that there are certain chords that indicate the end of a piece. The V chord resolving to the I chord heard in so many pop songs and in Bach and his cronies is called the perfect cadence. The good news is that rules are meant to be broken - hence Blues and Jazz and Metal and all sorts of other interesting genres.

Einstein's General Relativity, it didn't seem too much of a leap from Special Relativity, which itself was a straightforward extension from the ideas of Newton which I had learnt in school. Trying to explain it without following the history of ideas would be difficult. So think of your presentation as a story, a development of ideas or a route through your thought patterns. People like stories, and they will often skim slides in advance looking for the story. In the section on how to create great slides we will show how to make the story stand out simply - you can then fill in the detail during your presentation.

To control the presentation you need to control the environment. Make sure you know where the presentation will be, and try if possible to reconnoiter the room early to work out the layout of the seating, and where you are going to stand to ensure that the focus is on you. You should always stand if possible. *You* need to be the point of focus and there is no better way for doing this than being higher up and centrally located. Watch any great orator, presenter or performer, you will see them standing on a plinth or stage, above their audience, grab their attention and hold it to the rousing climax of their speech.

You should put everything in place to make sure that you are fully in control of the room and of the presentation. You set the pace, you decide when it starts and finishes and you decide who asks what questions and which ones you answer. Don't take questions during the talk as this disrupts the flow. The audience is yours for the duration of the presentation but you must keep them engaged, and focussed

on you and your message. This is the difficult bit, and we
will deal with this in the delivery section.

9.2 Creating slides for impact

Preparing the slides does not mean that you have prepared
the presentation.

If you must, then you must. 'Death by powerpoint' is
such a commonly used phrase that it must have some basis
in truth!! For me, powerpoint should be banned, but it
seems to be an evil necessity. We seem to be constrained
by the technology in to thinking in certain, very linear, slide
oriented way. There is a good reason for this structure, but
it makes every presentation similar, linear and quite frankly
boring. By throwing of the shackles of powerpoint oriented
thinking you have an opportunity to create something more,
but this can take courage. In this chapter we will be mothers
of convention, and won't push out the boat too much. We
are, after all consultants, and as such in the position where
we need to convey a message. From what we know about
rapport we know we should use understood and standard
professional mechanisms for the right effect.

This does not mean that we can't be creative, and can't
think of new ways of getting our point across. Certainly in
less formal presentation settings alternative approaches can
be extremely effective. In fact in formal settings unconven-
tional approaches can have a real impact, but you need to
be courageous and clear about your aims here. I urge you to
explore the fantastic *Presentation Zen* [Reynolds, 2008] for

a radical, and extremely effective approach to presentations that create an impression. We will look at some of the ideas here in relation to creating our own powerful presentations.

Slides should be an aide memoir, and should not contain all of the information around the main idea. Too many times have I attended presentations in which the presenter puts up a slide, and then reads each line on the slide verbatim. There is no point in that at all, you may as well just give out the slides (another bad idea[3]). The idea is to put key ideas and points on the slide to give you something to talk about. Think about them as a backdrop to your talk, not as the focal point, which should be you.

Don't be afraid to have lots and lots of slides. The best kind of slide has one idea, one clear message, and usually one picture, or other anchor, to illustrate the idea. The worst kind of slide has ten ideas and a gamut of supporting information and no pictures or other anchors. There is a basic limit to the capability of human memory and comprehension which is illustrated in well known research [Miller, 1956]. Miller shows that the basic capacity for retaining information is seven items, with nine being the very best case and five being the worse[4]. This means that if we wish to have someone remember key items from our presentation we should make our objective a maximum of seven big ideas.

---

[3]If you give out the slides then that encourages the impatient and curious in the audience to jump ahead of where you are. This both spoils any impact form key slides and also allows *them* to set the pace, and not you

[4]In my experience, during a presentation or even discussion five pieces of information seems at the limit of retention for most, especially when there is no real conscious effort being made to retain information.

You will notice in advertising and marketing and in politics that they have even less faith in our capacity to process lots of information and they usually keep big ideas to at most three. There is a good reason for this, for three well articulated and repeatable ideas become repeated, and are memes and anchors for the duration of a campaign. We all remember key advertising slogans and political messages. The idea is to make the idea big enough and simple enough, and to craft the language well enough to make not just the idea, but the way it is presented repeatable. And once someone says something, then they own it. *Vorsprung Durch Technic!!*

The good news is that the human mind has the capacity for chunking which means that we can remember and process more by grouping ideas. This is why telephone numbers are grouped. For example the number 01267 234 674 is three groups with each group of no more than four items which is easy to remember, and the sequence of the groups is also within our capacity. Compare this with trying to remember 01267234674. We can use this principle to structure or presentation in to a number of big ideas, which are groups of smaller ideas. This is the basic powerpoint approach of headings and bullets, it is not my favorite.

Headings on slides are bad, or at the very least pointless. Headings in books are necessary as they indicate what the chapter is about, but on slides they waste time, they tell you nothing, and you have to fill in the rest of the ideas with endless bullet points. To create presentations that really work, where you would have put the heading, you put the idea. For example where you may have put a slide like figure

9.1 :

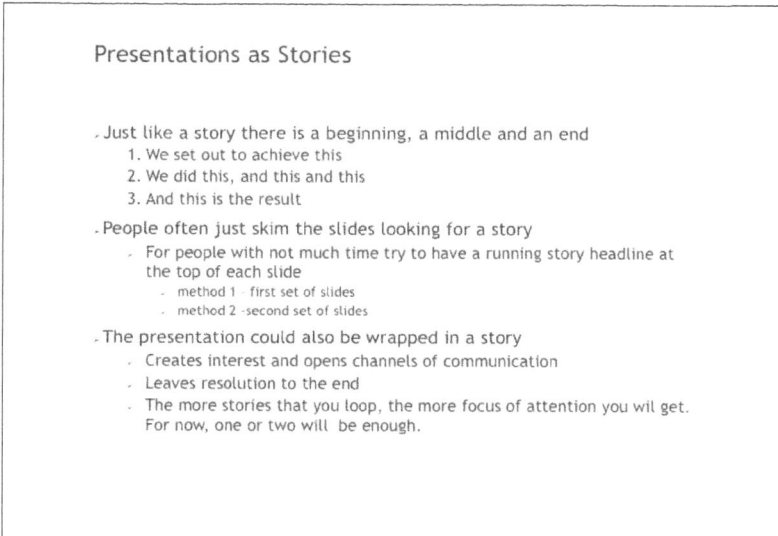

Figure 9.1 – Headings are bad

you instead would create the slide in fig 9.2:

This then allows the reader to grasp the main concept or message on the slide with out worrying about the supporting detail. This then means that the audience of the presentation can read along the top, or middle lines of the entire presentation and get the story that you are telling just from the headlines, rather than having to wade through lots of detail.

For example the following four slides (figures 9.3, 9.4,9.5,9.6) give you a flavour of this idea. Rather than read the detail in each slide, just focus on the headlines.

Though effective, I wonder though whether you notice just how boring these slides are? And more importantly just how unmemorable. A very powerful way of creating an

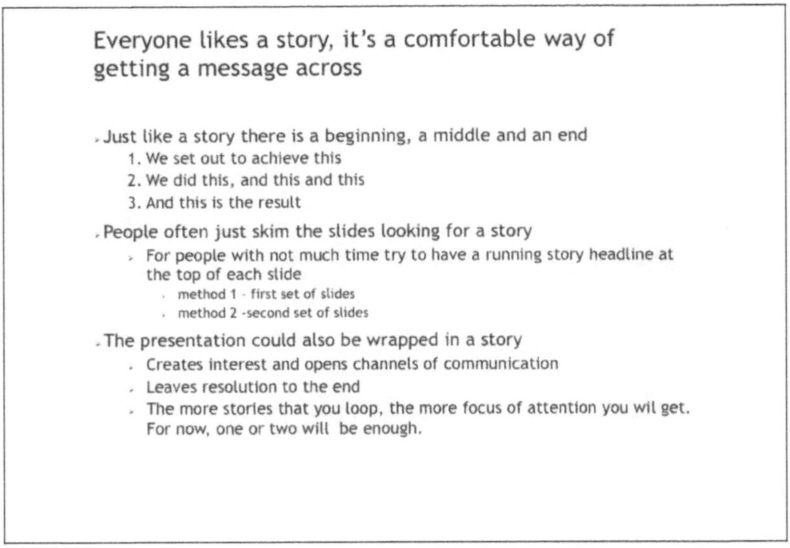

Everyone likes a story, it's a comfortable way of getting a message across

- Just like a story there is a beginning, a middle and an end
    1. We set out to achieve this
    2. We did this, and this and this
    3. And this is the result
- People often just skim the slides looking for a story
    - For people with not much time try to have a running story headline at the top of each slide
        - method 1 - first set of slides
        - method 2 -second set of slides
- The presentation could also be wrapped in a story
    - Creates interest and opens channels of communication
    - Leaves resolution to the end
    - The more stories that you loop, the more focus of attention you wil get. For now, one or two will be enough.

Figure 9.2 – An alternative approach to headings

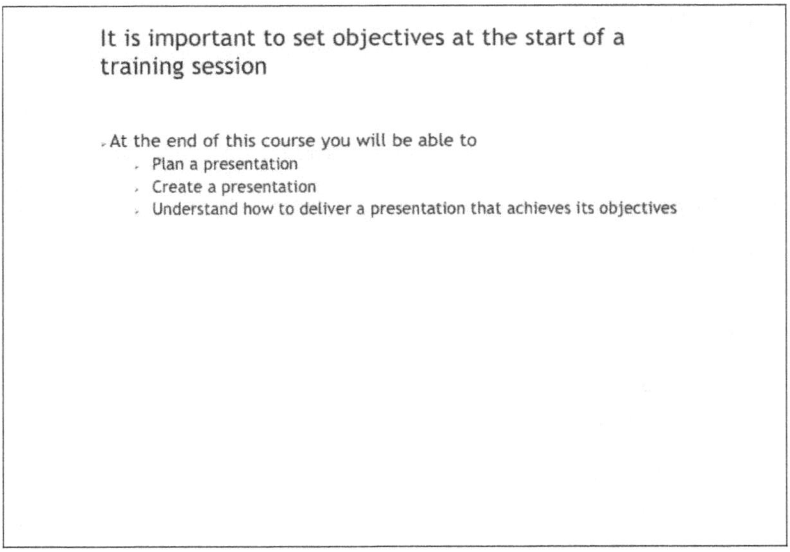

It is important to set objectives at the start of a training session

- At the end of this course you will be able to
    - Plan a presentation
    - Create a presentation
    - Understand how to deliver a presentation that achieves its objectives

---

Figure 9.3 – Headline slide 1 of 4

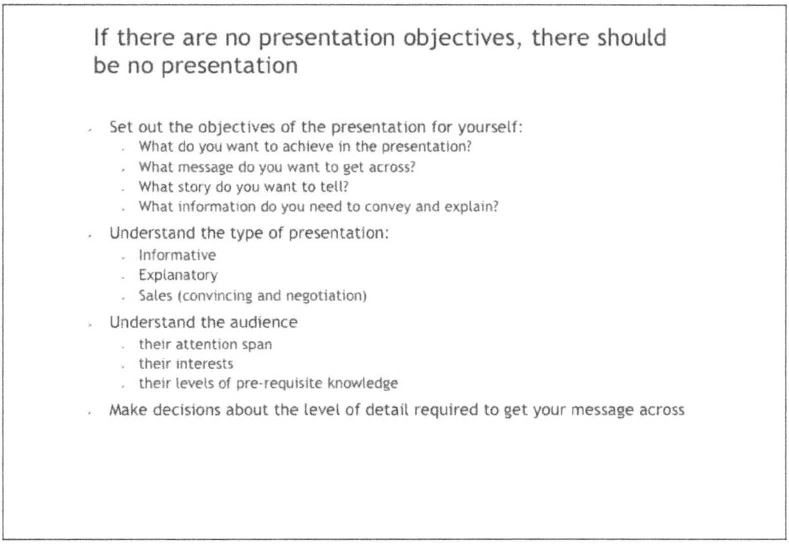

If there are no presentation objectives, there should be no presentation

- Set out the objectives of the presentation for yourself:
  - What do you want to achieve in the presentation?
  - What message do you want to get across?
  - What story do you want to tell?
  - What information do you need to convey and explain?
- Understand the type of presentation:
  - Informative
  - Explanatory
  - Sales (convincing and negotiation)
- Understand the audience
  - their attention span
  - their interests
  - their levels of pre-requisite knowledge
- Make decisions about the level of detail required to get your message across

Figure 9.4 – Headline slide 2 of 4

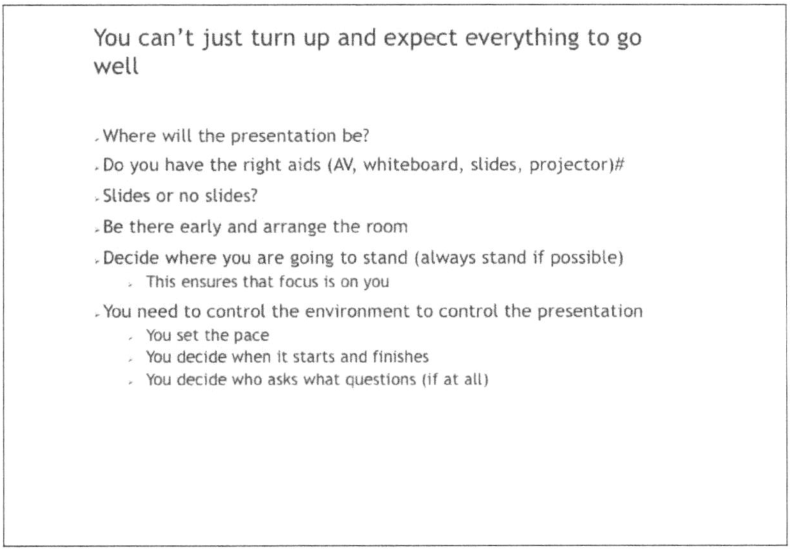

You can't just turn up and expect everything to go well

- Where will the presentation be?
- Do you have the right aids (AV, whiteboard, slides, projector)#
- Slides or no slides?
- Be there early and arrange the room
- Decide where you are going to stand (always stand if possible)
  - This ensures that focus is on you
- You need to control the environment to control the presentation
  - You set the pace
  - You decide when it starts and finishes
  - You decide who asks what questions (if at all)

Figure 9.5 – Headline slide 3 of 4

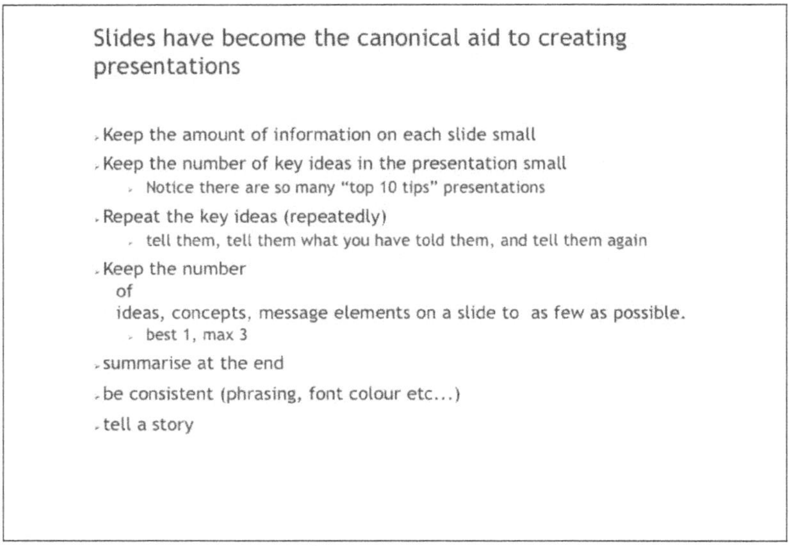

Figure 9.6 – Headline slide 4 of 4

Figure 9.7 – Adding a random picture to a slide

impact and helping to connect an anchor for a specific idea that you want to get across is to connect it with an image or picture.

There is a habit of adding a somewhat related picture to a slide almost as a way of keeping interest. Conservative as we are we may do something like figure 9.7

Here the picture of a dart in the bulls eye clearly invokes the ideas of targets and possibly objectives, but the connection is a bit of a stretch and all too often we just pick pictures because we need one and well 'that's about right'. We can use pictures in a much better way, to directly anchor concepts to really create an impact.

You can take a more bold approach and create a much bigger impact with pictures driving the message of the slide. Imagine figure 9.8 appearing in the middle of a presentation. Anyone who wasn't paying attention before, would now, and I would be prepared to put money on the fact that they will remember this slide, and as a result your presentation. For the best, most memorable and most impactful presentations, use large meaningful pictures and simple single messages for all slides.

In figures 9.9, 9.10, 9.11, 9.12 I have recreated the previous four slides (figures 9.3, 9.4, 9.5, 9.6) in a format that would be suitable for a *Zen presentation*. This may be too much for you, or for your client, so somewhere in between you will find a happy medium that creates impact, gets the message across and provides enough detail.

You will notice in the picture-oriented slides here that I haven't been overly consistent with font colour and size,

Figure 9.8 – Using pictures on slides for impact

but you will notice that the overall look and feel of the presentation is consistent. This, I think, is what we are aiming for, enough consistency to create a flow in the presentation but not so much that it becomes boring. The general rule is 'if in doubt - be consistent' and consistency is particularly important in slides that are more informational.

Margret Thatcher, a long running, successful and authoritarian conservative British Prime Minister once said of her presentations that they key to making sure that the audience understood her message was to 'tell them, tell them what you have told them, and tell them again'. There is merit in this and before you create your presentation make sure you know your key messages so that you can state them clearly in the presentation in such a way that the audience will take them in and repeat them to their colleagues,

Figure 9.9 – Zen slide 1 of 4

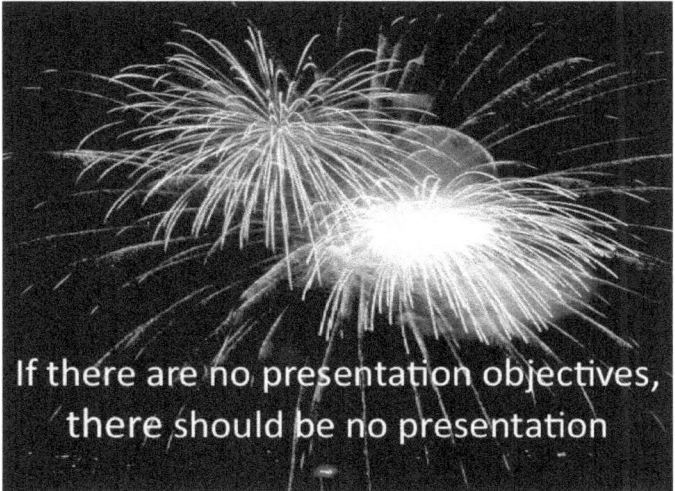

Figure 9.10 – Zen slide 2 of 4

Figure 9.11 – Zen slide 3 of 4

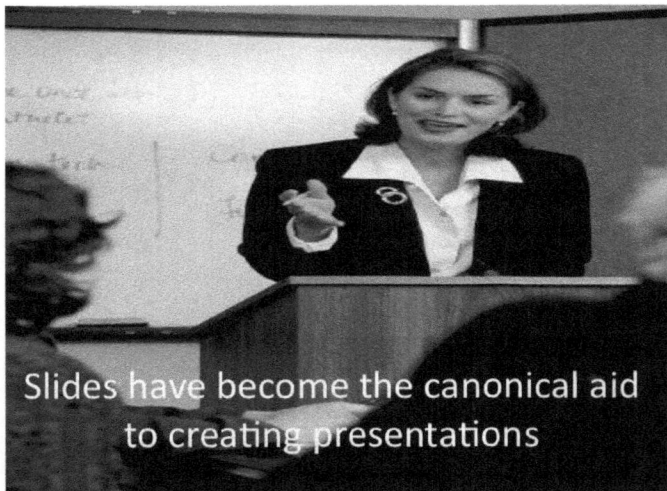

Figure 9.12 – Zen slide 4 of 4

friends and family when they leave. Once clarified, the ideas should be repeated, and then summarised at the end of the presentation. There will be far too much information given during your presentation, so ensuring that at the end you point out to the audience what the key takeaways are helps them know what they should remember.

To summarise then, here are the top tips for creating great presentation slides:

- No death by powerpoint.

- Prepare the slides and the presentation together. The former is not a substitute for the latter.

- Keep the number of key ideas in the presentation small.

- Repeat the key ideas, repeatedly.

- Keep the number of ideas, concepts, message elements on a slide to as few as possible, no more than three.

- If in doubt be consistent.

- Use images for impact and as anchors to ideas.

- Be courageous.

- Use the slides to tell a story.

- Summarise the key points at the end of the presentation.

9.3 Delivery - Being engaging

I have attended many presentations in which the presenter seems to be presenting to himself (which seems strange as he should already know the contents of the presentation), or to a select few audience members, completely disengaging the audience and ensuing that they miss the message[5] and only remember the presentation because it was one of the most boring they had ever attended. It your responsibility to *know your audience*, engage them and target your presentation for them.

Getting and keeping the right state

The presenter makes the presentation. In order to make a powerful presentation you need to be confident, in control of the audience and of yourself, to have a sense of personal power and capability, but not arrogance, and you need to make sure that you enjoy the experience just as much as the audience will. There are just a few ingredients to making sure that you come across as competent, passionate, engaging and capable. The first is to know your material, and know it well - know your message, and deliver it with confidence and passion.

You must also work to eliminate bad speaking habits, 'ums' and 'ers', repetitive phrases, unnatural pauses and anything that interrupts flow or takes attention away from the message. I'm sure you recall a time when you were

---

[5] I have attended equally many presentations where there was no message too...

listening to a speaker with a ticks or who used habitual phrases, and I am sure that you recall the tick or the habitual phrase very well, much better in fact than the content of the presentation. Many of these affectations are brought on by nerves, and some are deeply habitual. Nerves are relatively easy to deal with, habitual affectations possibly need specialist help[6] .

In general, you need to be in the right state (which is not 'a right state') for a presentation. And the right state is a *resourceful state*. We have already listed many of the key resources that you need - confidence, power, capability- and we could list a few more that would be useful - creativity, humor, fun - after all you need to enjoy the experience, and if you do your audience will also. The following device, the Power Circle, is a simple mechanism to help you get into a resourceful state and then call that state up at will. Doing it may take you out of your comfort zone, and if it does good... do it anyway and you will see, feel and hear the benefits as you step forwards to present, and in fact as you come to do anything for which a resourceful state is required.

The Power Circle

Try this exercise :

- Stand up, and imagine a circle on the ground with you at the centre. This circle should be sized so that if

---

[6]You may like to try a psychologist, hypnotherapist or personal coach, all of whom have effective habit breaking strategies that they can use to help.

you were to step forwards you would be stepping out of the circle. Can you see it? What colour is it?

- Now stand with your feet together in the centre of the circle, and imagine yourself calm and relaxed. Take yourself back to a time when you were particularly calm and relaxed. See what you saw then, hear what you heard, and feel what you felt at your most relaxed. This is the centre.

- Now step forwards into stance outside of the circle, and imagine yourself confident and powerful. Take yourself back to a time when you felt that confident, that powerful. See what you saw then, hear what you heard, and feel what you felt. Notice the sensations on your body. This is to the outside.

- Now step back in , and as you do recall those centre feelings, feelings of relaxation and calmness. Intensify those feelings as you step. Now step forwards, into stance, and as you do recall those sensations of being outside, confident, powerful, fast. Take those feelings and double them, intensify them.

- Now continue to step backwards and forwards, constantly changing your state from calm and centred, to powerfully, confidently outside the circle. Every time you do this double the intensity of the feelings. How do you feel now?

- And this time as you step forwards squeeze your right

hand just at the peak of intensity. Step back and fore-words into the power circle and do this three times. Each time squeezing your hand at the peak of intensity.

- Now think of something else, anything, a watermelon perhaps. How do you feel now? Now squeeze your hand. How do you feel now?

- You should feel resourceful and powerful and confident. If you need to feel enjoyment and fun, just repeat the process and add the resources you need

Make sure that you feel good every time you step forward or backward. You need to have the sensation of you stepping being your anchor. This concept, the concept of anchor comes from an application of the work of Pavlov around the turn of the century. He was a Russian scientist from the behaviourist school who demonstrated the power of stimulus-response theory by conditioning dogs to respond as if they were about to be fed, when they heard a bell ring. He did this by ringing the bell just before he fed them. Dogs salivate when they think of food, and eventually when Pavlov rang the bell and didn't deliver food, the dogs still salivated.

There are many times and places where we as humans respond in the same way to specific stimulus. For example, isn't there a particular song (normally known as 'our-song' by couples!!) which triggers particular memories and thoughts? Or doesn't the sight of a particular person fill you with dread? A very severe case of anchoring is a phobia in which the very sight of the tiniest spider can make an otherwise fearless person run and scream. And if we don't think that we are as unsophisticated as Pavlov's hungry canines, how many of us remember all too vividly the school bell!!

Anchors are relatively straightforward to create and can be in any form - a word, a picture, a sound, a movement. They have to be unique for each state that you want to access and they have to be a single item. In the case of phobias you only have to see the stimulus (spider) one time and respond (run and scream) in the way you did on that first occurrence, to generate a strong anchor or any time you see a spider in the future. The power circle exercise creates an anchor for all of the resourceful states you need before you start your presentation. Squeezing your hand is a shortcut to generating all of the states when you need them.

We can use anchors powerfully as we are presenting too, comedians use this particularly well. I once was at an Eddy Izzard show where he used this device to great effect. He told a hilarious joke early on in the proceedings, the punch line of which was 'in my mind'. Everyone laughed, and he milked it. Every time he wanted to get a laugh he just said the phrase 'in my mind' and connected it with random other jokes. The audience laughed, he fired the anchor. At the end of the show he went off stage to riotous applause and was called back for encore. Eventually he ran back on and just said that one phrase 'in my mind' and the auditorium exploded in laughter.

CHAPTER 9. POWERFUL PRESENTATIONS

Eddy created a state of enjoyment, fun and laughter and then anchored it with the words 'in my mind'. You can do a similar thing. I always start any presentation by talking about the presentations in general in my pre-amble, asking the audience (not overtly, I will normally do this in a jokey way, trying to create a sense of fun) to think back to a brilliant presentation where they learned lots and paid attention for the entire time, and then I will anchor that feeling with a key word or action. This means that I have already put the audience in a receptive state, and when I really want the audience to pay attention and have even more fun all I have to do is fire the anchor[7].

Anchors can be words, actions or spatial. You want the audience to have good feelings about you, the presenter, and by using a combination of humor and clarity in explanation you can create those feelings and then anchor them to you. That's right, *you* can become the anchor. This has an implication for you if your presentation isn't going well, in which case you become a bad anchor. If you have to make a presentation at a conference where you are following someone who has done a bad, boring, confusing, non-fun presentation then your audience will be in a pretty low state, and not feeling particularly receptive. You need to change this by creating a new set of resourceful states and anchors.

Of course the presenter himself, and what he said and did, were the main bad anchors and he is no longer there. There would however be other anchors around the room including where he was standing, a lecturn if there was one,

---

[7]Of course this will effect only the majority of the audience.

and the screen where the slides were shown. The first thing that you must do is stand somewhere else, not where the previous presenter was standing, this is the biggest spatial anchor. Move around if you can and create good anchors in other parts of the room. You can't do much about the slide screen, except have brilliantly impactful slides that are engaging and support, not drive, your presentation. Now that you know about anchors, you can think about them as you prepare and go through your presentation. Remember, they are not just for you!!

Using stories

One of the best way to create resourceful states in your audience is through the use of stories. Stories create rapport, they engage the audience, generate state and generate a sense of anticipation. They create interest and open channels of communication. Stories have been used for millennia as ways of communicating strong messages. Just look at the power of folklore, fairy stories, and the bible as really good examples[8]. Stories can take an average presentation and make it great. Your story can be a directly relevant true (or almost true) story that illustrates something of importance, or it can be a story that seems less relevant initially but contains a powerful message or generates a powerful state. I often tell the following story when I am giving training.

Napoleon was fighting a campaign in Russia when his army was routed. His headquarters came under attack and

---

[8]This book is also full of stories for good reason.

he was forced to hide. He ran to a friendly village and found himself inside a furriers cottage. He could hear the Russian troops coming closer and so the furrier told him to hide under one of the big piles of furs. The Russians burst in and started prodding the furs with their bayonets, getting closer and closer to the pile that Napoleon was under. The furrier was clearly getting very nervous. Just then French troops ran in and, after a fire fight, killed the Russians, rescuing Napoleon. The battle had turned and the french were again on top. The furrier looked at Napoleon as he emerged from beneath the furs and asked him 'You must have been terrified, they almost had you. What does it feel to be that close to death?' Napoleon seemed angered by the question and he marched the furrier outside, assembled a firing squad, had him tied to a post and blindfolded.

Pausing stories is a device that can be used to maintain attention. Right now, for example, if you want to know the end of the story you have to skip down a paragraph. If you were in a presentation you wouldn't be able to do this, and so your attention would be wrapped and whatever I sandwiched in between the start and finish of the story would be given your full attention. This is a common device and the more stories you start the more the audience will be waiting for the resolution, and will pay close attention. We all need resolution. Starting stories within stories is known as looping, and is a device used by great orators when they want to deliver messages powerfully and persuasively. The middle of a looped story is a great place to insert suggestions if you feel that you want to make your message really stick.

This is why advertisements are placed in the middle of a film.

The furrier was terrified, he heard the powder and balls being dropped into the muzzles, he heard the order to prepare and the click of the mechanism as the guns were cocked. Then nothing... He waited and he heard steps coming towards him, crunching on the gravel. They came closer and then stopped. The blindfold was removed and he looked straight into the face of Napoleon who said... 'Now, you know'.

There are many possible interpretations for this story, and I will leave it to you to find the one that makes more sense to you in this context. You can find a good source of stories that you could use to wrap a presentation in Parkin [2001] although you will have to tailor them for your audience.If you search on the internet you will find many stories of various quality. Don't forget your own experiences, true stories resonate more deeply.

The final thing to think of is the use of your voice. In delivery of a presentation your voice should be clear and powerful but not shouting. It should be commanding and confident but not arrogant. You should have gravitas, more like Winston Churchill than Joe Pasquali. You achieve this by having good posture, ensuring you are confident and in control and speaking from your stomach, not your chest and not your nose. Practice. When you speak put your hand on your stomach, you want to be able to feel it vibrate. Try and move the vibration down by speaking from your lower abdomen. This contributes more than anything else to your presence, and to your ability to command the room.

These presentation skills are in addition to your general communication skills and your ability to create rapport with a group, which we discussed in section 6.2.1. You have everything you need and so now, the rest is down to you. I am not going to wish you luck, as it is not luck you need, it is skill and capability and attitude and preparation and practice. Go for it!!

So the boy captured the bird and ran back to the village with it in his hands. When he got to the wise man, he asked his question. 'Wise man, is what I have in my hands dead or alive?' And the wise man, as wise men tend to do, thought for a few moments, his legs crossed, playing with his long grey beard. After some time, he smiled and with a grin on his face he answered the little boy: 'well...', he said 'It is, evidently, all in your hands'.

CHAPTER 9.   POWERFUL PRESENTATIONS

Chapter 10

The Consultant as an agent of change

This is a very short chapter. It just contains some advice. Since it it so short, you might like to read it anyway. It won't take long.

Heisenberg's uncertainly principle is one of the fundamental principles of quantum mechanics[1], which states fundamentally that you can't measure or observe something without changing it. This doesn't just apply to elementary particles. We can perhaps feel sorry for Schrödingers cat, in a box with a vial of poison which will kill it instantly if the box is opened. We don't know whether the cat is alive or dead, but if we open the box to find out, there is only one answer. Just like Schrödinger, you must accept that by engaging in consultancy, however unobtrusive, you effect the

---

[1]If you are interested in the pholosophical implications of the strange world of elementary particles in the quantum domain you might like to seek out the very readable 'in search of Schrödingers Cat' by John Gribbin

outcome. That difference you make is connected to what you ask, who you ask, what you do and when you do it and who you do it with, and hopefully no small furry animals die as a result.

This is your purpose. When you are engaged as a consultant you are engaged in order to provide advice, get something done, deliver and achieve an outcome. In whatever way, in fact just by being there you are changing the organisation and the people in it. This is the case for all of us, but as a masterful consultant you now have a toolbox of skills which can help you create even more influence, more direction and a greater sense of momentum. You are now a powerful an agent of change. And with great power comes great responsibly.

Some of the tools in your toolbox are power tools, and they should be used wisely. All tools can be used to make things but equally they can be used to break things. If you hit your thumb, or worse, somebody else's thumb, with a hammer, don't blame the hammer.

Your tools of negotiation and influence are there to help you help the organisation achieve their outcomes, and they are there to help you to achieve your outcomes. Think carefully about how and where you apply these tools and remember that the most important thing is that as an agent for change you are facilitating change, lead by the client, not driving your agenda. As a consultant you don't know best, but you do know how to get the best out of your clients and their organisation. Use your toolkit with integrity. Try not to hit your thumb.

There were two caterpillars sitting on a leaf, chatting. A butterfly flew overhead. One caterpillar turned to the other and said 'you'll never get me up in one of those'.

Consultancy is one of the best jobs in the world. There is lots of variety, the pay is good and more than anything you are the difference that makes a difference. Enjoy being an agent of change.

Chapter 10. The Consultant as an agent of change

Part III

Supplementary Material

Presuppositions

Scattered throughout the text there are a set of statements that will help you to look at the world in a way that helps to create a framework for exquisite communication and ultimately better consultancy. They are a set of fundamental principles that are known in the NLP community as *presuppositions*.

1. We are always communicating.

2. The meaning of the communication is the response that you get.

3. People respond to their map of reality, not to reality itself.

4. The element in a system with the most flexibility will usually be the controlling element.

5. People always make the best choice available to them.

6. Every behavior is useful in some context.

7. Experience has a structure. Anything can be accomplished if we break it down into small enough pieces.

8. People already have most of the resources that they need.

9. There is no failure, only feedback.

10. If what you're doing does not work, do something else.

Meeting guidelines

The seven golden rules

As we discussed in the text, meeting planning is essential to the success of any meeting. When you start the meeting, however, you need to remember the following seven golden rules to ensure that the meeting gets the result that you require.

1. Stick to the agenda.

2. No AOB.

3. Stick to the time frame.

4. Stick to the objective (Either gain agreement on the decision or on a agreement to take actions that will help gain agreement).

5. State and agree actions.

6. Always create minutes.

7. Stick to the agenda.

Meetings - the order of things

Meetings are pretty linear, and if you run them right they will be entirely linear in as much as each section - *introduction, decision, summary, followup* - all have to happen in order. The following list is am aide memoir to this order and the things yo should focus on at each stage.

1. Start on time.

2. Gain and maintain rapport with all participants.

3. State the objective.

4. State all roles.

5. Explain the agenda and how you are going to achieve the objective.

6. Follow the pack (agenda).

7. Follow the seven golden rules.

8. Finish on time (or early).

9. Summarise.

10. State the decision.

11. State the actions.

12. Minute.

Well Formed Outcomes and Requirements

Capturing requirements or stating consultancy outcomes is one thing, but all too often we find that there is a gap between what is required and what is achievable. This is avoidable by making sure that in the process of establishing the requirement or outcome efforts are made to make sure that they satisfy the well formedness criteria.

What do you want? Rather than asking what the problem is, ask the client to state what they want. They should state it in positive terms. Ask 'What do you want, and what do you want it to do?', 'Where do you want it? When do you want it?'. If it is something that they do not want, then ask, 'What do you want instead of...?'

Can you achieve it? Is it possible to achieve the outcome? If someone else or some other system has done it, then in theory the client can do it too. If this is the first time that it is to be done find out if it is possible.

What will you accept as evidence that the outcome or

requirement has been achieved. What are the criteria for a successful test? What evidence will he client accept that lets them know when they have achieved it? Ensure this is expressed in clearly in terms of what they will be able to see, hear and do once the outcome or requirement is achieved. This is the equivalent of the 'Measurable' criteria in the SMART outcome test.

Is achieving this outcome within your control? Is it under their control, or your control. Ask 'Can you, personally do, authorise or arrange it?' Anything outside of their control is not *well formed*.

Do you have all the resources you need to achieve this outcome? Can you, or the client have or can they obtain all the resources, both tangible and intangible, that they need to achieve their outcome? Resources include knowledge, beliefs, objects, premises, people, money, time...

What will happen when you have succeeded? There may be consequences that have not yet been thought of. For example, if the outcome is to automate a process, this may cause upheval through role change or redundancy in the team. This is known as an ecology check. Consider the costs, consequences, environmental impact and effect on others after having achieved the outcome.

Proposals Do's and Don'ts

When you are writing a proposal, there are a number of things to remember. The most important of these is that the proposal supports the sale, but is not a sales document. Here are the full list:

Proposals should:

- Stipulate the outcomes of the project.

- Describe how progress will be measured.

- Establish accountabilities.

- Set the intended start and stop dates.

- Provide methodologies to be employed.

- Explain options available to the client.

- Convey the value of the project.

- Detail the terms and conditions of payment of fees and reimbursements.

- Serve as an ongoing template for the project.

- Establish boundaries to avoid 'scope creep'.

- Protect both consultant and client.

- Offer reasonable guarantees and assurances.

Proposals should not:

- Sell the interventions being recommended.

- Create the relationship.

- Serve as a commodity against which other proposals are compared.

- Provide the legitimacy and/or credentials of your firm and approaches.

- Validate the proposed intervention.

- Make a sale to a buyer you have not met.

- Serve as a negotiating position.

- Allow for unilateral changes during the project.

- Protect one party at the expense of the other.

- Position approaches so vaguely as to be immeasurable and unenforceable.

Presentation checklist

The three keys to a great presentation are: preparation; message; and presence. This checklist will help you make sure that you are thinking about the right things as you create your plan and then execute it. You will notice that the first half of this list concern presence, as this is the most important and most evident skill in delivery.

- Have relevant and appropriate stories.

- Have control of your environment.

- Have control of yourself.

- Have confidence.

- Speak clearly.

- Have the correct voice tone.

- Be in the right state.

- Bring the focus of the audience to *you*.

- Make sure that the audience are in a receptive state.

- Have a simple and clear message.

- Have well crafted and clear visual aids.

- Ensure that you end the presentation with a resolution.

Remember, even more than all of this, *have fun*.

Bibliography

Richard Bandler. *Frogs Into Princes*. Real People Press, 1977. This is an essential read, exploring the magic of representation systems amongst other things. The style of Bandler and Grinder takes a little getting used to though.

Richard Bandler. *Trance-Formations*. Meta Publications, 2008. A valuable text that includes all of the basic skills for building rapport and creating powerful language patterns, as well as effecting personal change.

Richard Bandler and John Grinder. *The Structure of Magic*. Real People Press, 1979. This is the book that started the revolution. As Richard Bandler's PhD essentially it defines many of the linguistic principles behind excellence in communication and development of the tools and techniques of NLP. Its quite technical so not for the feinthearted.

Richard Bandler and John LaValle. *Persuasion Engineering*. Meta Publications, 1996. This is Bandler's best book, it is clear, lucid and although written in his usual discursive style, is more readable than others. The focus is on sales and influence and there are lots of great examples to help clarify the approach.

BIBLIOGRAPHY

Robert Cialdini. *Influence: The Psychology of Persuasion.* Harper Business, 2007. The seminal work on the science of influence. A must read.

Stephen R. Covey. *The 7 Habits of highly effective people.* 1989. An excellent book that outlines what you need in order to be excellent at your job, and in life. In particular it has one of the best sections on time management that I have come accross.

Jaques Derrida. *Writing and Difference.* University of Chicago Press, 1980. A postmodern classic that pre-empted many of the later social constructivist ideas which have lead to a human centered way of looking at knowledge. Its academic and terse, and is worth a look from an historical point of view or if you want to understand more clearly some of the deep thinking about the ways in which we come to understand things.

Roger Fisher and William L Ury. *Getting to Yes: Negotiating agreement without giving in.* Penguin Group, 1981. This text focusses on the Psychology of negotiation and is the outcome of the Harvard negotiation project. The approach taken in non-adversarial, and moves towards compromise. There are some excellent examples taken form high level, real life conflict and negotiation experiences.

Daniel Goleman. *Emotional Intelligence: Why it can matter more than IQ.* Bloomsbery, 1996. The concept of EI was first articulated and developed in this book. It sometimes comes in for criticism, but the general principles are sound and worth digesting and considering.

Genie Laborde. *Influencing WIth Integrity.* Crown House, 2001. An excellent guide to the process of building rapport, and some fantastic tips on the art of influence.

George Miller. The magic number seven plus or minus two: some limits on our capacity for processing information. *The Psychological Review*, 63(2):81–87, 1956. Written over 60 years ago and still referred to as a key psychological principle. You don't need to read this paper as it is summarised in many places, but the devil is in the detail and if you have some time it is worth investigating Miller's reasoning first hand.

Margret Parkin. *Tales for Coaching: Using Stories and Metaphors with individuals and small groups.* Kogan Page., 2001. A great source of stories. Useful for any situation, and easy to incorporate in any presentation. Valuable to have in your collection.

Garr Reynolds. *Presentation Zen.* New Riders Press, 2008. This is a fantastic book that will change the way that you think about presentations forever. Have courage.

Martin van Creveld. *Command in War.* Harvard University Press, 1985. One of my favourite books, from which I have derived many valuable management techniques and approaches that have served me well. Its also really very well written and contains thoroughtly interesting analysis

of command in Napolean's campaigns and the Vientam
war.

Alan Weiss. *Getting Started In Consulting*. Wiley, 2003.
Alan Weiss has written many books on consulting, mainly
from the perspective of the independant consultant. This
one is an excellent addiiton to your library and gives great
tips for starting out as a consultant. In particular this book
has valuable chapters on value based pricing and proposal
writing.

Index

www.ingramcontent.com/pod-product-compliance
Lightning Source LLC
Chambersburg PA
CBHW021557210326
41599CB00010B/477